Classically
INSPIRED

Classically INSPIRED

A Celebration of British Food

EVANS BROTHERS LIMITED

GARDNER MERCHANT

Published by Evans Brothers Limited
2A Portman Mansions
Chiltern Street
London W1M 1LE

First published in 1996

ISBN 0 237 51656 X

Acknowledgements
Classically Inspired is a collaboration of the many skills of a dedicated
Gardner Merchant team:
Peter Hazzard, Executive Director, Food Services
Julia Newton, Food Services Development Manager
John Whybrew, Food Services Development Chef
Paul Burton, Senior Craft Training Manager
Philippa Carter, National Merchandising Co-ordinator
Andi Redwood, Craft Training Manager
Peter Joyner, Craft Training Manager
Jackie Neave, Craft Training Manager
Tony Robertson, Craft Training Manager
Anne Simpson, Chief Dietician

The Gardner Merchant team would also like to thank the following for their
help and support in the publication of *Classically Inspired*:
Vicky Hanson, Editor, Stylist
Ivor Innes, Photographer
Neil Sayer, Designer
Our celebrity chefs for their inspiration:
Anton Edelmann
Anton Mosimann
Paul and Jeanne Rankin
Gary Rhodes
Franco Taruschio
Antony Worrall Thompson
Gardner Merchant's Chef's Circle for recipe ideas
The Cheese Cellar Company for supplying cheeses and information

The following recipes and photographs were reproduced by kind
permission of the publishers:
Brill with Asparagus and Tomato and Herb Dressing – Pavilion Books Ltd
Tenderloin of Welsh Lamb with Herbs and Grain Mustard – Ebury Press Ltd
Boiled Collar of Bacon with Home-Made Sauerkraut – BBC Books
Blackened Monkfish with Curried Aubergine – Mitchell Beazley
Lady Llanover's Salt Duck with Pickled Damsons –
photograph, Express Newspapers; recipe Pavilion Books Ltd
Photograph of Gary Rhodes – Anthony Blake Photo Library

CONTENTS

FOREWORD

Gardner Merchant's history spans over 110 years and our heritage lies in traditional British food. Now, as a truly international company, we felt it apt to celebrate this heritage with this book of delicious recipes.

Many of the great chefs today have been inspired by classic British cooking, with versions of steak and kidney pudding, Lancashire hotpot and summer pudding appearing with increasing regularity on the menus of the top restaurants.

In our own organisation, where we serve over two million meals a day, we find that the British classics are as popular as ever, but it is the chefs' flair that makes them particularly special – the dishes they create are 'classically inspired'. In this book we have brought together a selection of the best recipes from our highly skilled chefs. Many have a contemporary feel but they all include the best of British ingredients.

At Gardner Merchant we are always keen to learn, and throughout 1995 we ran a number of Master Classes where our own chefs worked with Anton Edelmann, Anton Mosimann, Paul and Jeanne Rankin, Gary Rhodes, Franco Taruschio and Antony Worrall Thompson to acquire new skills and to produce a gourmet dinner to celebrate the quality of British food. Some of the classically inspired recipes created by these chefs are featured in this book for you to try for yourself.

We hope you will enjoy making these dishes for your family and friends as much as our customers have enjoyed eating them.

Happy cooking!

Garry Hawkes
Executive Chairman
Gardner Merchant

REDISCOVERING THE CLASSICS

Over the last 20 years or so, classic British recipes have lost favour to dishes from around the world, influenced by the increasing popularity of holidays abroad and by the many restaurants opening in our high streets – Italian, Chinese, Indian and American eateries are now commonplace, tempting our palates with the delights of their national cuisines. As more and more books featuring these recipes become available, we often entertain our guests with dishes we have discovered while visiting these restaurants or on holiday.

As a result, here in Britain we are in danger of losing a culinary heritage as rich as that of any other country. *Classically Inspired* aims to rediscover British recipes and bring them into the 1990s. The emphasis in this book is on adding a contemporary feel to the classics as well as introducing innovative new recipes made from British ingredients. The book includes a selection of everyone's favourites, with easy-to-follow recipes to remove the mystique of preparing professional-looking dishes in your own home. All the ingredients are easy to find and many, especially the fresh meat and fish, can be bought ready prepared.

MASTER CLASSES

Unique to *Classically Inspired* are the recipes from celebrity chefs. Throughout 1995 Gardner Merchant held 'Master Classes' run by a number of top chefs and based on the theme 'A celebration of the quality and diversity of British Food'. Working alongside Anton Edelmann, Anton Mosimann, Paul and Jeanne Rankin, Gary Rhodes, Franco Taruschio and Antony Worrall Thompson, Gardner Merchant's own chefs learnt the new skills necessary to produce all the elements of spectacular gourmet meals which were then served to specially invited guests.

Master Class 95 was a huge success. The Gardner Merchant chefs learnt many new ideas to take back and inspire their own staff, while the dinner guests experienced food of an outstanding quality that would be difficult to surpass in any of the top restaurants. A selection of the dishes featured in the Master Classes is included in this book so now you, too, have the opportunity to try some of their recipes.

THE RECIPES

The book is divided into simple chapters featuring recipes for all occasions, including breakfast and afternoon tea, those two great institutions for which the British are renowned the world over. Try our delicious, simple-to-follow recipes and discover a whole host of classic dishes to add to your repertoire.

In addition to the recipes is a guide to our national cheeses, with suggestions for putting together different cheeseboards to help you discover the variety of high quality cheeses produced in Britain.

To complete this collection of British classics is an inspiring chapter on Entertaining which puts together menus based on the recipes featured in the book. There are also lots of ideas to make your entertaining stress-free, with hints on planning and time-saving suggestions, so you can enjoy the occasion as much as your guests.

SUCCESSFUL COOKING

Alongside the recipes are useful tips to help you save time and to ensure successful results, as well as imaginative serving suggestions and variations on the basic recipes. We couldn't write a recipe book concerned with cooking in the 1990s without referring to the time-saving devices and ingredients that are now widely available. Food processors and blenders, for example, are commonplace in the domestic kitchen and can be invaluable to the cook, whether preparing a supper dish for two or a buffet for twenty. References are also made to good-quality, ready-prepared ingredients such as frozen puff pastry and chilled stocks.

The key to success when cooking any dish is to remember that you don't have to stick rigidly to the recipe – ingredients, equipment and oven temperatures can all vary, so keep tasting the dish as it cooks and use your own judgement to adjust the seasoning or cooking time to achieve the best results.

When following the recipes in this book, please note the following:

Measurements are given in metric with their imperial equivalents in brackets. Follow one set only, do not mix the two measurements in one recipe.

All eggs are size 3 unless otherwise specified.

All spoon measurements are level. A teaspoon is 5 ml, a dessertspoon is 10 ml and a tablespoon is 15 ml.

All herbs are fresh unless otherwise specified. If you replace fresh herbs with dried, use only half the amount specified.

BREAKFASTS

KEDGEREE

❖

SCRAMBLED EGG WITH ANCHOVIES

❖

CHICKEN LIVERS WRAPPED IN SMOKED
BACON

❖

PORK AND LEEK SAUSAGES

❖

BLACK PUDDING WITH FIELD
MUSHROOMS, POACHED EGG AND APPLE
SLICES

❖

DROP SCONES WITH BUTTER AND WARM
HONEY

❖

STEWED BREAKFAST FRUITS

❖

FRUITY PORRIDGE

KEDGEREE

A favourite Victorian breakfast dish from the days of the raj. It's now popular at any time of the day.

INGREDIENTS TIP
Arborio rice is an Italian, short-grained variety that is used in risottos. It gives the kedgeree a deliciously creamy texture.

INGREDIENTS FOR 4 SERVINGS

175 g (6 oz)	SMOKED HADDOCK
300 ml (½ pint)	MILK
600 ml (1 pint)	VEGETABLE STOCK
3 tablespoons	OLIVE OIL
1	SMALL ONION, FINELY CHOPPED
1	GARLIC CLOVE, CRUSHED
1 teaspoon	CHOPPED FRESH THYME
100 g (4 oz)	ARBORIO RICE
	GRATED ZEST AND JUICE OF ½ LEMON
2 teaspoons	MILD CURRY SAUCE
2 teaspoons	GRATED PARMESAN CHEESE
2	HARD-BOILED EGGS
	SALT AND FRESHLY GROUND BLACK PEPPER
	FINELY CHOPPED FRESH PARSLEY, TO GARNISH

Put the haddock and milk in a saucepan, bring slowly to the boil and poach for 5 minutes, until the fish is just cooked. Drain and leave to cool. Remove the skin and bones and flake the flesh.

Meanwhile, bring the stock to the boil in a large saucepan and keep at a simmer. Heat the oil in a saucepan. Add the onion, garlic and thyme and cook gently for 3 minutes until soft but not coloured. Add the rice and stir until the grains are coated in the oil.

Increase the heat and add a cupful of the hot stock. Cook, stirring, until the rice has absorbed the liquid. Add another cupful of stock and cook, stirring, until absorbed. Add the remaining stock and cook briskly, stirring, for about 15 minutes. Stir in the lemon zest and juice and curry sauce. Chop one of the hard-boiled eggs. Reserve a few flakes of fish for garnish and add the remainder to the pan with the Parmesan cheese, chopped egg and seasoning. Stir and heat gently to warm through.

To serve, transfer to a warmed serving dish or arrange in mounds on warmed serving plates. Arrange the reserved fish flakes on top. Push the reserved egg through a sieve over the kedgeree. Garnish with parsley and serve.

Overleaf:
Kedgeree

SCRAMBLED EGG WITH ANCHOVIES

Chopped anchovies really liven up a plate of creamy scrambled eggs.

INGREDIENTS FOR 4 SERVINGS

25 g (1 oz) BUTTER

8 EGGS, BEATEN

2 teaspoons DOUBLE CREAM

4 ANCHOVY FILLETS, FINELY CHOPPED

SALT AND FRESHLY GROUND BLACK PEPPER

Gently melt the butter in a non-stick saucepan. Add the eggs and cook over a gentle heat, stirring constantly, until lightly scrambled.

Remove the pan from the heat and stir in the cream and anchovies. Season, remembering that anchovies are quite salty, and serve immediately.

> **COOKING TIP**
> Be careful not to overcook the eggs – they continue to cook in their own heat so they should still be creamy when you remove the pan from the stove.

CHICKEN LIVERS WRAPPED IN SMOKED BACON

A classic savoury dish that makes an interesting addition to a cooked breakfast.

INGREDIENTS FOR 4 SERVINGS

4 CHICKEN LIVERS

4 RINDLESS, SMOKED STREAKY BACON RASHERS

Pre-heat the grill. Trim the chicken livers, removing any discoloured or white parts. Place a chicken liver on to each bacon rasher and neatly roll up.

Grill, turning once, until the bacon is golden and crisp and the chicken livers are still pink in the centre. Serve immediately.

PORK AND LEEK SAUSAGES

Why not try making your own sausages; it's really quite easy and the flavour is so much better than most commercial ones.

> **COOKING TIP**
> If the mixture seems too wet, add some more breadcrumbs.

INGREDIENTS FOR 4 SERVINGS

150 ml (¼ pint) CHICKEN STOCK
50 g (2 oz) LEEK, FINELY SHREDDED
350 g (12 oz) MINCED PORK
100 g (4 oz) SHREDDED BEEF SUET
GRATED ZEST OF 1 LEMON
1 teaspoon FINELY CHOPPED FRESH SAGE
15 g (½ oz) PLAIN FLOUR
1 tablespoon FRESH WHITE BREADCRUMBS
1 EGG, BEATEN
SALT AND FRESHLY GROUND BLACK PEPPER
VEGETABLE OIL FOR FRYING

Bring the stock to a rapid boil, add the leek and blanch for 20 seconds. Remove with a slotted spoon and drain on kitchen paper. Leave to cool.

Put all the remaining ingredients except the oil in a bowl and beat together thoroughly. Add the cooled leeks.

Divide the mixture into four and, on a lightly floured surface, roll the mixture into neat sausages. Heat the oil in a frying pan and gently shallow fry the sausages for 15–20 minutes until browned all over and cooked through.

VARIATIONS

If you prefer, pipe the mixture into a sausage skin, twisting the skin between each sausage to form links. You can buy sausage skin from most butchers.

Experiment with different ingredients and flavours. Add some finely chopped bacon or apple, herbs such as sage, thyme, mint or parsley, grated lemon zest, or English mustard.

A classic cooked English breakfast can include all kinds of savoury items.

BLACK PUDDING WITH FIELD MUSHROOMS, POACHED EGG AND APPLE SLICES

A contemporary version of a traditional cooked breakfast that's equally delicious served for lunch.

INGREDIENTS FOR 4 SERVINGS

4	EVEN-SIZED FIELD MUSHROOMS OR OPEN-CUP MUSHROOMS
15 g (½ oz)	MELTED BUTTER
25 g (1 oz)	LARD OR BACON FAT
4	SLICES BLACK PUDDING
15 g (½ oz)	BUTTER
2	EATING APPLES, PEELED, CORED AND SLICED
1 tablespoon	MALT VINEGAR
4	EGGS
	FRESHLY GROUND BLACK PEPPER
	PARSLEY SPRIGS, TO GARNISH

Pre-heat the grill. To prepare the mushrooms, remove the stalks and carefully peel the caps. Put the mushrooms on a baking sheet, brush with melted butter and cook under a moderate grill for 10 minutes, turning once.

Meanwhile, melt the lard in a frying pan, add the black pudding and fry for 3 minutes on each side.

Melt the butter in a small frying pan and gently cook the apple slices until just soft and beginning to turn a golden brown.

Bring a saucepan of water to a gentle simmer then add the vinegar. Carefully crack the eggs into the water and poach gently for about 3 minutes until the whites are just set (you may find it easier to poach just two eggs at a time).

To serve, place a mushroom, cup side uppermost, on each warmed serving plate and top with a slice of black pudding. Place a poached egg on top. Arrange the apple slices at the side. Season generously with coarsely ground black pepper, garnish with parsley sprigs and serve.

Black Pudding with Field Mushrooms, Poached Egg and Apple Slices

DROP SCONES WITH BUTTER AND WARM HONEY

Warm, sweet little pancakes that just melt in your mouth.

INGREDIENTS FOR 10–12 SCONES

100 g (4 oz)	SELF-RAISING FLOUR
2 tablespoons	CASTER SUGAR
1	EGG, BEATEN
150 ml (¼ pint)	MILK
50 g (2 oz)	BUTTER, MELTED
	VEGETABLE OIL FOR FRYING
	BUTTER AND WARMED CLEAR HONEY, TO SERVE

Sift the flour into a bowl and stir in the sugar. Mix together the egg and milk. Make a well in the flour and add the egg and milk mixture. Gradually stir the flour into the liquid to form a smooth batter. Stir in the melted butter.

Lightly oil a griddle or heavy-based frying pan and heat. Drop three or four spoonfuls of the batter on to the griddle to form small pancakes. Cook for 1–2 minutes until bubbles appear on the surface of the scones. Turn the scones over and cook for a further 1–2 minutes until golden on both sides. Stack the scones on top of one another and keep warm while cooking the remaining batter.

Serve the pancakes with butter and warmed honey.

STEWED BREAKFAST FRUITS

A rich mixture of dried fruits, delicious topped with natural yogurt.

> **INGREDIENTS TIP**
> Ready-to-eat dried fruits are more expensive, but don't need soaking if you're in a hurry.

INGREDIENTS FOR 4 SERVINGS

450 g (1 lb)	MIXED DRIED PRUNES, APRICOTS, PEACHES AND APPLES
	STRIP OF LEMON ZEST
	STRIP OF ORANGE ZEST
1 tablespoon	DEMERARA SUGAR
	NATURAL YOGURT, TO SERVE

Wash the fruit, place in a bowl with 600 ml (1 pint) water and leave to soak overnight.

Put the fruit, water and sugar into a saucepan with the lemon and orange zest. Bring to the boil and simmer for about 40 minutes until tender. Remove the fruit with a slotted spoon and transfer to a serving bowl.

Boil the cooking liquor until it is reduced and syrupy, then strain over the fruit. Serve hot or cold, with natural yogurt.

FRUITY PORRIDGE

A warming dish of creamy porridge topped with fruit and nuts.

INGREDIENTS FOR 4 SERVINGS

175 g (6 oz) ROLLED OATS
300 ml (½ pint) WATER
300 ml (½ pint) MILK
2 tablespoons DOUBLE CREAM
1 tablespoon CLEAR HONEY

FOR THE TOPPING

25 g (1 oz) GLACE CHERRIES, SLICED
25 g (1 oz) RAISINS
15 g (½ oz) NIBBED ALMONDS

Put the oats, water and milk into a saucepan and bring slowly to the boil, stirring all the time. Simmer for 4–5 minutes. Remove from the heat and stir in the cream and honey.

Pour into serving bowls, top each serving with a few cherries, raisins and a sprinkling of nuts and serve immediately.

SOUPS AND STOCKS

GREEN PEA AND HAM SOUP

Commonly called 'London Particular', after the thick London fogs that came to be known as pea-soupers.

SERVING TIP
Serve this soup with multi-coloured bread: Soften 50 g (2 oz) butter and blend with 25 g (1 oz) finely chopped watercress. Spread between 5 slices of bread (3 brown and 2 white) and sandwich the slices together, alternating the breads. Remove the crusts, wrap in cling film and chill. Slice and serve.

INGREDIENTS FOR 4 SERVINGS

225 g (8 oz)	FRESH OR FROZEN PEAS
1	ONION, CHOPPED
1	LEEK, CHOPPED
600 ml (1 pint)	HAM STOCK
65 g (2½ oz)	BUTTER
65 g (2½ oz)	PLAIN FLOUR
600 ml (1 pint)	MILK
50 ml (2 fl oz)	DOUBLE CREAM
100 g (4 oz)	COOKED HAM, FINELY DICED
	SALT AND GROUND WHITE PEPPER

Put the peas, onion, leek and stock into a saucepan. Bring to the boil and simmer for 15 minutes. Drain, reserving the stock.

Meanwhile, melt the butter in a saucepan, add the flour and cook, stirring, for 1 minute. Gradually stir in the milk and reserved stock and heat gently, stirring, until thickened. Reduce the heat and simmer for 10 minutes.

Reserve a few whole peas for garnish and put the remainder in a food processor with the onion and leek and process until smooth. Pass through a sieve. Stir the vegetable purée into the milk mixture with the cream and heat gently to warm through. Adjust the seasoning. Ladle the soup into warmed bowls, add the ham and reserved peas and serve.

VARIATION

A wide range of soups can be made using this white sauce as a base. Replace the peas and ham with broccoli and almonds, or watercress and cooked chopped bacon.

Overleaf:
Green Pea and
Ham Soup

CULLEN SKINK

A traditional Scottish soup that makes a filling lunch dish.

INGREDIENTS FOR 4 SERVINGS

350 g (12 oz)	SMOKED HADDOCK
600 ml (1 pint)	MILK
600 ml (1 pint)	FISH STOCK
1	ONION, FINELY DICED
450 g (1 lb)	MASHED POTATOES
25 g (1 oz)	BUTTER
15 g (½ oz)	FINELY CHOPPED FRESH PARSLEY
	SALT AND GROUND WHITE PEPPER

Put the haddock, milk, stock and onion in a saucepan, bring slowly to the boil and simmer for 5 minutes. Remove the fish and leave to cool. Strain the milk into a clean saucepan.

Remove the skin and bones from the fish and flake the flesh with a fork. Add the fish to the strained milk and stock then stir in the mashed potatoes and butter to give a thick, creamy consistency. Heat gently to warm through. Stir in the parsley, season to taste and serve in warmed bowls.

SERVING TIP
Pour the soup into individual ovenproof soup cups and leave to cool. Roll out 100 g (4 oz) puff pastry to 5 mm (¼ inch) thick and cut out four rounds, 5 mm (¼ inch) larger than the top of the soup cups. Lightly score the pastry lids with a knife and brush evenly with egg yolk. Put on top of the soup cups and pierce the pastry to allow the steam to escape. Bake at 190C/375F/Gas 5 for 10–15 minutes until the pastry is risen and golden and the soup is warmed through.

CELERY AND STILTON SOUP

The distinctive flavour of Stilton complements so well the more subtle, fresh taste of celery.

INGREDIENTS FOR 4 SERVINGS

350 g (12 oz)	CELERY
50 g (2 oz)	BUTTER
1	ONION, ROUGHLY CHOPPED
50 g (2 oz)	PLAIN FLOUR
1.1 litres (2 pints)	VEGETABLE OR CHICKEN STOCK
1	BAY LEAF
50 g (2 oz)	MATURE STILTON CHEESE, CRUMBLED
	SALT AND GROUND WHITE PEPPER
4	SPRIGS OF CHERVIL AND SINGLE CREAM, TO GARNISH

Wash the celery and divide into sticks, reserving four of the smaller central sticks. Roughly chop the remaining celery. Melt the butter in a large saucepan, add the onion and celery and stir to coat with the butter. Cover and allow the vegetables to sweat for 5 minutes, until soft but not coloured.

Add the flour and cook, stirring, for 1 minute. Gradually stir in the stock and heat gently, stirring, until thickened. Add the bay leaf and simmer for 20 minutes, stirring from time to time.

Remove the bay leaf, transfer the soup to a food processor or blender and process until smooth. Return to the saucepan and heat gently to warm through. Add the Stilton and stir until incorporated. Season to taste.

Thinly slice the reserved celery sticks and add to the soup 2 minutes before serving, so they retain a slight crispness.

To serve, transfer the soup to warmed bowls, swirl a little cream in each one and garnish with chervil sprigs.

MINTED CUCUMBER AND HONEYDEW MELON SOUP

A delightfully light and refreshing combination of summer flavours.

INGREDIENTS FOR 4 SERVINGS

1 LARGE HONEYDEW MELON
½ CUCUMBER
GRATED ZEST AND JUICE OF ½ LEMON
25 g (1 oz) CASTER SUGAR (OPTIONAL)
15 g (½ oz) FRESH ROOT GINGER, PEELED AND FINELY CHOPPED
600 ml (1 pint) WATER
3 LARGE SPRIGS OF MINT, CRUSHED
SALT AND GROUND WHITE PEPPER
MINT LEAVES, TO GARNISH

> **COOKING TIP**
> Always adjust the seasoning of a cold dish when it is thoroughly chilled, as cold food tends to need more seasoning than foods served hot.

Cut the melon in half, remove the seeds, then cut the flesh into quarters. Use a melon baller to make 12 small melon balls and reserve for garnish. With a sharp knife, cut the remaining flesh from the skin. Roughly chop the flesh and put in a large saucepan.

Peel the cucumber and roughly chop. Add to the saucepan. Add the lemon zest, caster sugar, if using, ginger and water and stir well. Bring to the boil, cover and simmer for 10 minutes. Add the mint sprigs and leave the soup to cool.

Discard the mint sprigs, transfer the soup to a food processor or blender and process until smooth. Season and add lemon juice to taste. Cover and chill for at least 2 hours, preferably overnight.

To serve, adjust the seasoning and serve the soup in chilled bowls, garnished with the reserved melon balls and mint leaves.

GOLDEN VEGETABLE SOUP

An attractive clear soup with strips of colourful vegetables, cooked until just tender. The turmeric gives the soup its rich golden colour.

COOKING TIP
It is very important to have a good quality vegetable stock (see page 35) to give this soup the best flavour.

INGREDIENTS FOR 4 SERVINGS

25 g (1 oz) BUTTER

1 GARLIC CLOVE, CRUSHED

1 ONION, SLICED

½ teaspoon GROUND TURMERIC

25 g (1 oz) WHITE BUTTON MUSHROOMS, HALVED AND SLICED

1 LARGE CARROT, CUT INTO MATCHSTICKS

2 CELERY STICKS, CUT INTO MATCHSTICKS

100 g (4 oz) SWEDE, CUT INTO MATCHSTICKS

100 g (4 oz) PARSNIPS, CUT INTO MATCHSTICKS

100 g (4 oz) CAULIFLOWER, BROKEN INTO SMALL FLORETS

25 g (1 oz) FROZEN PEAS

900 ml (1½ pints) VEGETABLE STOCK

SALT AND GROUND WHITE PEPPER

Melt the butter in a large saucepan, add the garlic and cook, stirring, for 1 minute. Add the onion and turmeric and cook, stirring, for 2 minutes. Add all the vegetables except the peas and cook gently for 10 minutes, stirring occasionally.

Pour in the stock and add the peas and seasoning. Bring to the boil and simmer for 2 minutes. Season to taste and serve.

VARIATION

This soup can be made with a good quality chicken stock (see page 32) and garnished with fine shreds of cooked chicken.

Golden Vegetable Soup

LEEK AND POTATO SOUP

An all-time favourite that can be served hot or chilled.

<table>
<tr><td colspan="2">COOKING TIP</td></tr>
</table>

COOKING TIP
Summer-style soups should be thick enough to just coat the back of a spoon; winter soups usually have a thicker consistency.

INGREDIENTS FOR 4 SERVINGS

25 g (1 oz)	BUTTER
225 g (8 oz)	LEEKS, WHITE PARTS ONLY, CHOPPED
1	LARGE ONION, CHOPPED
225 g (8 oz)	POTATOES, DICED
600 ml (1 pint)	CHICKEN STOCK
300 ml (½ pint)	MILK
	SALT AND GROUND WHITE PEPPER
150 ml (¼ pint)	SINGLE CREAM
	FINELY CHOPPED WATERCRESS, TO GARNISH

Melt the butter in a large saucepan, add the leeks and onion and cook, stirring occasionally, for 5 minutes, until soft but not coloured. Add the potatoes, stock and milk. Bring to the boil, cover and simmer for 20 minutes.

Transfer to a food processor or blender and process until smooth. Return to the pan, stir in the cream and season to taste. Heat gently to warm through. Ladle into warmed serving bowls, garnish with watercress and serve.

VARIATION

Leave the soup to cool after stirring in the cream. Chill thoroughly, season and serve in chilled bowls.

HEARTY VEGETABLE SOUP

A rich, winter-time soup flavoured with curry powder.

INGREDIENTS FOR 4 SERVINGS

1 tablespoon	OLIVE OIL
1	ONION, CHOPPED
225 g (8 oz)	MIXED CARROTS, POTATOES AND PARSNIPS, DICED
225 g (8 oz)	MIXED CELERY, FENNEL AND GREEN PEPPER, DICED
1	GARLIC CLOVE, CRUSHED
1 teaspoon	MILD CURRY POWDER
1	BAY LEAF
900 ml (1½ pints)	VEGETABLE STOCK
425 g (14 oz)	CAN BUTTER BEANS, DRAINED
2 tablespoons	FINELY CHOPPED FRESH PARSLEY
	SALT AND FRESHLY GROUND BLACK PEPPER

FOR THE GARNISH

1	SLICE WHITE BREAD, CRUSTS REMOVED
	VEGETABLE OIL FOR DEEP FRYING
4	SAVOY CABBAGE LEAVES, FINELY SHREDDED

Heat the oil in a large saucepan, add the onion and diced vegetables and cook, stirring occasionally, for 5 minutes, until soft but not coloured. Add the garlic, curry powder and bay leaf and cook, stirring, for 2 minutes. Add the stock. Bring to the boil, cover and simmer for 20 minutes.

Add the beans and cook for 5 minutes. Discard the bay leaf, transfer half the soup to a food processor or blender and process until smooth. Return the purée to the soup in the saucepan. Stir in the parsley, season to taste and heat gently to warm through.

To make the garnish, cut the bread into 5 mm (¼ inch) cubes. Heat the vegetable oil in a deep-fat fryer or large saucepan to 180C/350F. Deep fry the bread cubes until golden brown. Remove with a slotted spoon and drain on kitchen paper. Add the shredded cabbage to the oil and deep fry for a few seconds until crisp. Remove with a slotted spoon and drain on kitchen paper.

To serve, ladle the soup into individual warmed bowls, pile a little fried cabbage on top and scatter with the fried bread.

SMOKED CHICKEN AND AVOCADO SOUP

This unusual marriage of flavours makes an ideal summer starter that looks delightful with its garnish of crisp, fried vegetables. Serve in avocado shells for an unusual presentation.

SERVING TIP
If you haven't time to prepare the garnish, simply finish the soup with a sprinkling of snipped chives.

INGREDIENTS FOR 4 SERVINGS

100 g (4 oz) SMOKED CHICKEN BREAST, CUBED
3 RIPE BUT FIRM AVOCADOS
JUICE OF ½ SMALL LIME
SALT AND GROUND WHITE PEPPER
900 ml (1½ pints) COLD CHICKEN STOCK

FOR THE GARNISH

1 SMALL LEEK, WHITE PART ONLY, SHREDDED
1 SMALL CARROT, SHREDDED
PARED ZEST OF 1 SMALL LIME
VEGETABLE OIL FOR DEEP FRYING
SALT
150 ml (¼ pint) SINGLE CREAM
MINT SPRIGS
DRIED CHILLI FLAKES

Reserve a quarter of the chicken for garnish. Halve and stone the avocados and scoop out the flesh, leaving a thin layer in the shell and putting the shells to soak in salted water if using for serving.

Put the chicken, avocado, lime juice and seasoning in a food processor or blender. Process until smooth, gradually adding the stock. Transfer to a bowl, cover and chill.

To make the garnish, mix together the leek, carrot and lime zest. Heat the oil in a deep-fat fryer or large saucepan to 180C/350F. Deep fry the leek mixture for a few seconds until crisp. Remove with a slotted spoon and drain immediately on kitchen paper. Season with salt.

To serve, drain the avocado shells, if using. Pour the soup into the shells or individual chilled bowls, add the reserved chicken cubes and swirl in a little cream. Place a small dome of the fried leek mixture on top, garnish with mint and chilli flakes and serve.

Smoked Chicken and Avocado Soup

CHICKEN STOCK

A versatile stock that can be used in all kinds of dishes – fish and vegetable as well as poultry.

COOKING TIPS
Don't add salt when making a stock, it is best if seasoned according to the dish it is used in.

All types of stock freeze well. Divide into smaller quantities before freezing – 600 ml (1 pint) is probably most convenient.

INGREDIENTS FOR 2.3 LITRES (4 PINTS)

50 g (2 oz) BUTTER
2 ONIONS, SLICED
2 CELERY STICKS, SLICED
2 LEEKS, SLICED
1.8 kg (4 lb) CHICKEN CARCASSES, CHOPPED
3.4 litres (6 pints) WATER
FEW PARSLEY STALKS
1 BAY LEAF
1 SPRIG OF THYME
8 BLACK PEPPERCORNS

Melt the butter in a stockpot or large saucepan. Add the vegetables and cook, stirring, for 3 minutes until soft but not coloured.

Add the remaining ingredients and bring to the boil, skimming any scum from the surface. Simmer for 2–3 hours, regularly skimming the surface. Strain the stock, discarding the bones, vegetables and herbs and use as required.

BEEF OR VEAL STOCK

The classic method for producing a richly flavoured, meaty stock.

INGREDIENTS FOR 3.4 LITRES (6 PINTS)

25 g (1 oz)	LARD
3	ONIONS, HALVED
3	CELERY STICKS, ROUGHLY CHOPPED
3	CARROTS, ROUGHLY CHOPPED
1	LEEK, ROUGHLY CHOPPED
2.3 kg (5 lb)	VEAL OR BEEF BONES, CHOPPED
5.7 litres (10 pints)	WATER
	FEW PARSLEY STALKS
1	BAY LEAF
1	SPRIG OF THYME

Pre-heat the oven to 200C/400F/Gas 6. Put the lard in a roasting tin and put in the oven for about 10 minutes until the lard is hot. Add the vegetables and turn to coat in the lard. Put the bones in another roasting tin and roast with the vegetables for 30–40 minutes until browned.

Transfer the vegetables and bones to a stockpot or large saucepan and add the water and herbs. Bring to the boil, skimming any scum from the surface. Simmer for 6–8 hours.

Strain the stock, discarding the bones, vegetables and herbs and use as required.

VARIATION

To produce a jus, which condenses the flavours, boil the stock after straining until reduced to 600 ml (1 pint), skimming the surface to remove any impurities. This will naturally thicken the stock.

BUYING TIPS

Ask your butcher to chop the bones for you when you buy them.

A home-made stock is really in a league of its own, but if you don't have the time to make it, the best commercial ones are the fresh, chilled stocks found in most large supermarkets.

FISH STOCK

The simplest and quickest of all the stocks.

INGREDIENTS FOR 2.3 LITRES (4 PINTS)

50 g (2 oz)	BUTTER
1	ONION, SLICED
1	LEEK, SLICED
3	CELERY STICKS, SLICED
900 g (2 lb)	WHITE FISH BONES AND WHITE FISH SKIN
300 ml (½ pint)	DRY WHITE WINE
2.3 litres (4 pints)	WATER
	FEW PARSLEY STALKS
6	BLACK PEPPERCORNS
1	BAY LEAF

Melt the butter in a stockpot or large saucepan. Add the vegetables and cook, stirring, for about 3 minutes until soft but not coloured. Add the fish bones and skin and cook for 2 minutes.

Add the wine and boil until almost all the wine has evaporated. Add the water, parsley stalks, peppercorns and bay leaf. Bring to the boil and simmer for 20 minutes. Strain the stock, discarding the trimmings, vegetables and herbs and use as required.

VEGETABLE STOCK

A light stock that adds flavour to all kinds of soups and sauces.

INGREDIENTS FOR 1.1 LITRES (2 PINTS)

25 g (1 oz) BUTTER
225 g (8 oz) CARROTS, DICED
4 CELERY STICKS, DICED
1 ONION, CHOPPED
2 LEEKS, CHOPPED
1 BAY LEAF
1 SPRIG OF THYME
FEW PARSLEY STALKS
1.1 litres (2 pints) WATER

> **INGREDIENTS TIP**
> Other vegetables, such as tomatoes or mushrooms, can be added to this stock, but don't use cabbage as it has too strong a flavour, or potatoes, as they will make the stock cloudy.

Melt the butter in a stockpot or large saucepan, add the vegetables and herbs and cook, stirring occasionally, for about 10 minutes until soft but not coloured.

Add the water and bring to the boil, skimming any scum from the surface. Simmer for 30 minutes. Strain the stock, discarding the vegetables and herbs, and use as required.

STARTERS

POACHED PEARS WITH STILTON

❖

SPINACH AND CAERPHILLY TERRINE

❖

WARM WATERCRESS, POTATO AND CRISPY
BACON SALAD

❖

SMOKED HADDOCK AND CHIVE FISHCAKES

❖

TARRAGON-STUFFED MUSHROOMS

❖

SOMERSET BRIE AND SMOKED SALMON
PARCELS

❖

POTTED CHEESE WITH HERBS

❖

SOUSED HERRINGS

❖

LADY LLANOVER'S SALT DUCK WITH
PICKLED DAMSONS

POACHED PEARS WITH STILTON

The tangy Stilton sauce contrasts well with the refreshing fruit in this mouth-watering starter.

<table>
<tr><td>

PREPARATION TIP
A melon baller is ideal for scooping out the core of each pear half.

</td></tr>
</table>

INGREDIENTS FOR 4 SERVINGS

4 PEARS, PEELED

WATERCRESS SPRIGS, TO GARNISH

FOR THE FILLING

100 g (4 oz) WATERCRESS, TRIMMED AND FINELY CHOPPED

175 g (6 oz) STILTON CHEESE, GRATED OR CRUMBLED

225 ml (8 fl oz) MAYONNAISE

Cut the pears lengthways in half and carefully remove the cores. Cut in half again to give four quarters, leaving the stalk on one quarter, if possible. Poach gently in a small amount of water for 2–5 minutes, depending on the ripeness of the pears, until just tender. Drain and leave to cool.

To make the filling, put the watercress in a bowl, add the Stilton and mayonnaise and mix well to combine.

To serve, pre-heat the grill. Put the cooled pear quarters on to individual heatproof serving plates, spoon over the cheese mixture and put under a hot grill until golden. Garnish with watercress.

VARIATION

Stilton is a very strong flavoured cheese. If you prefer, reduce the quantity of cheese or use a milder cheese, such as Shropshire Blue.

Overleaf:
Poached Pears
with Stilton

SPINACH AND CAERPHILLY TERRINE

A rich and creamy starter – not for the faint-hearted!

INGREDIENTS FOR 8 SERVINGS

2 teaspoons	OLIVE OIL
2	SPRING ONIONS, FINELY CHOPPED
2	GARLIC CLOVES, CRUSHED
175 g (6 oz)	FRESH SPINACH LEAVES
225 g (8 oz)	CAERPHILLY CHEESE
2	EGGS
	SALT AND FRESHLY GROUND BLACK PEPPER
200 ml (7 fl oz)	DOUBLE CREAM

INGREDIENTS TIP
This terrine can be made with other British cheeses, such as Cheshire or Wensleydale.

Pre-heat the oven to 180C/350F/Gas 4. Lightly oil a 1.1 litre (2 pint) ovenproof terrine or loaf tin and line the base and sides with baking parchment.

Heat the olive oil in a frying pan, add the spring onions, garlic and spinach and cook, stirring gently, until the spinach has wilted and all the liquid has evaporated. Transfer the spinach mixture to a food processor or blender, add the Caerphilly, eggs and seasoning and process until smooth. Stir in the cream.

Pour the mixture into the prepared terrine and cover with greased foil. Put the terrine in a roasting tin and pour in sufficient boiling water to reach halfway up the sides of the terrine. Cook in the oven for 1½ hours.

Remove the terrine from the roasting tin and leave to cool. Carefully pour off any excess liquid and chill for at least 2 hours, or overnight if preferred.

To serve, hold a serving plate over the terrine and carefully invert to turn out the terrine. Remove the baking parchment and cut the terrine into slices.

WARM WATERCRESS, POTATO AND CRISPY BACON SALAD

The hot and cold ingredients in this salad make a wonderful combination. Serve as a starter or light snack.

INGREDIENTS TIP
If black mustard seeds are unavailable, you could replace the prepared mustard with wholegrain mustard, although the dressing will not have such a strong flavour.

INGREDIENTS FOR 4 SERVINGS

450 g (1 lb) BABY NEW POTATOES, SCRUBBED
4 RASHERS RINDLESS BACK BACON, CUT INTO LARGE STRIPS
1 bunch WATERCRESS, TRIMMED

FOR THE DRESSING

3 tablespoons VEGETABLE OIL
1 tablespoon WHITE WINE VINEGAR
1 teaspoon PREPARED ENGLISH MUSTARD
1 teaspoon BLACK MUSTARD SEEDS
SALT AND FRESHLY GROUND BLACK PEPPER

Cook the potatoes in a saucepan of boiling salted water for 10–15 minutes until tender. Pre-heat the grill. Grill the bacon for 5 minutes until golden and crisp.

Meanwhile, make the dressing. Combine the oil, vinegar, mustard and mustard seeds in a saucepan and heat gently, stirring constantly. Season and remove from the heat.

To serve, drain the cooked potatoes and cut in half. Place in a warmed serving dish. Add the crispy bacon and watercress and pour over the warm dressing. Toss well to ensure all the ingredients are coated in the dressing. Serve warm.

VARIATION
To turn this dish into a special light meal, add a poached egg to each serving and serve immediately.

Warm Watercress, Potato and Crispy Bacon Salad

SMOKED HADDOCK AND
CHIVE FISHCAKES

The best of British ingredients combine in these crisp, golden cakes.

SERVING TIPS
Double the quantities and serve as a main course.

Serve with a Tartare Sauce (see page 54).

INGREDIENTS FOR 4 SERVINGS

50 ml (2 fl oz)	MILK
200 g (7 oz)	SMOKED HADDOCK FILLET
2 teaspoons	LEMON JUICE
1 teaspoon	WORCESTERSHIRE SAUCE
1 teaspoon	CREAMED HORSERADISH
2 teaspoons	SNIPPED FRESH CHIVES
2 teaspoons	FINELY CHOPPED FRESH PARSLEY
100 g (4 oz)	MASHED POTATOES
	SALT AND FRESHLY GROUND BLACK PEPPER
25 g (1 oz)	FRESH WHOLEMEAL BREADCRUMBS
	MIXED SALAD LEAVES, TO SERVE

Put the milk and fish in a shallow pan, cover with a sheet of baking parchment and bring slowly to the boil. Reduce the heat so the liquid is just simmering and poach the fish for 5 minutes. Drain, reserving the milk, and leave to cool.

Remove the skin and any bones from the haddock. Put the haddock in a food processor with the lemon juice, Worcestershire sauce and horseradish and process until smooth. Alternatively, use a fork to mash together all the ingredients.

Stir in the reserved milk, chives, parsley, potatoes and seasoning. Shape the mixture into four fishcakes and coat with the breadcrumbs. Pre-heat the grill. Cook under a moderate grill for 5 minutes on each side, or until lightly browned.

Serve immediately, on a bed of salad leaves.

TARRAGON-STUFFED MUSHROOMS

Lightly grilled mushrooms with a creamy sauce that has the aromatic flavour of tarragon and the tang of wholegrain mustard.

INGREDIENTS FOR 4 SERVINGS

4	LARGE OPEN-CUP MUSHROOMS
25 g (1 oz)	BUTTER
1 tablespoon	PLAIN FLOUR
150 ml (¼ pint)	MILK
2 teaspoons	WHOLEGRAIN MUSTARD
2 teaspoons	FINELY CHOPPED FRESH TARRAGON
150 ml (¼ pint)	SOURED CREAM
	MIXED SALAD LEAVES, TO SERVE

Remove the stalks from the mushrooms and peel the caps. Melt the butter in a saucepan. Put the mushrooms on a baking sheet and brush with some of the melted butter. Set aside.

Stir the flour into the remaining melted butter and cook, stirring, for 1 minute. Remove from the heat and gradually stir in the milk, to make a smooth sauce. Return to the heat and cook gently, stirring, until the sauce thickens. Simmer for 2 minutes. Remove from the heat and stir in the mustard, tarragon and soured cream.

Meanwhile, pre-heat the grill. Grill the mushrooms for 3 minutes, turning once, until warmed through.

To serve, arrange the salad leaves on serving plates and add the mushrooms. Spoon over the tarragon sauce and serve immediately.

VARIATION
The sauce can be flavoured with a variety of different herbs, such as chives, coriander or basil.

SOMERSET BRIE AND SMOKED SALMON PARCELS

Cut open one of these crispy breadcrumbed parcels and you'll find a luscious filling of melting Brie.

INGREDIENTS FOR 4–6 SERVINGS

50 g (2 oz)	SOMERSET BRIE
115 g (4½ oz)	SMOKED SALMON
	VEGETABLE OIL FOR DEEP FRYING
	FLOUR FOR DUSTING
1	EGG, BEATEN
	BREADCRUMBS FOR COATING
	SALAD LEAVES, TO SERVE

FOR THE DRESSING

4 tablespoons	GRAPESEED OIL
1 tablespoon	BALSAMIC VINEGAR
1 tablespoon	ELDERBERRY CORDIAL
	SALT AND FRESHLY GROUND BLACK PEPPER

Cut the Brie into twelve equal portions. Cut the salmon into 24 strips. Form two strips of salmon into a cross and put a piece of Brie in the centre. Fold over one strip of salmon. Working clockwise, continue folding over the salmon until the Brie is enclosed. Repeat with the remaining Brie and smoked salmon to give twelve parcels.

Heat the oil in a deep-fat fryer to 180C/350F. Dust each parcel with flour then dip in beaten egg and coat with breadcrumbs, making sure they are well covered.

Lower into the hot oil, in batches, and cook for 3 minutes until golden. Drain on kitchen paper and keep warm. Meanwhile, make the dressing. Put the oil, vinegar, cordial and seasoning in a screw-top jar and shake well to combine.

To serve, arrange the salad leaves on serving plates, put two or three parcels on each plate and pour over a little of the dressing.

Somerset Brie and Smoked Salmon Parcels

POTTED CHEESE WITH HERBS

A rich starter that is best followed by a light main course. It's also great for picnics or buffets.

INGREDIENTS FOR 4 SERVINGS

175 g (6 oz) MATURE CHEDDAR CHEESE, GRATED

50 g (2 oz) STILTON CHEESE, CRUMBLED

4 tablespoons DOUBLE CREAM

3 tablespoons DRY SHERRY

2 tablespoons FINELY CHOPPED FRESH PARSLEY, THYME, CHIVES AND TARRAGON

SALT AND GROUND WHITE PEPPER

SLICES OF WALNUT BREAD, TO SERVE

Put the cheeses and cream into a bowl and put the bowl on top of a saucepan of simmering water. Heat, stirring, until the cheese has melted and combined with the cream. Stir in the sherry and herbs. Season, then pour the mixture into four individual ramekins.

Leave to cool, then cover and chill. To serve, spread on to slices of walnut bread.

VARIATION

Try serving potted cheese as an unusual alternative to a cheese board at the end of a meal.

SOUSED HERRINGS

These marinated fish fillets can be prepared well in advance, in fact the longer they're left, the better they taste.

INGREDIENTS FOR 6 SERVINGS

6	HERRING FILLETS
1 tablespoon	SALT
2 teaspoons	ENGLISH MUSTARD
2	DILL PICKLES, THINLY SLICED
1	SMALL ONION, THINLY SLICED

FOR THE MARINADE

1 teaspoon	ALLSPICE BERRIES
½ teaspoon	MUSTARD SEEDS
1 teaspoon	CORIANDER SEEDS
1	FRESH RED OR GREEN CHILLI, SEEDED AND CHOPPED
2	FRESH BAY LEAVES
2 teaspoons	BROWN SUGAR
300 ml (½ pint)	WHITE WINE VINEGAR
150 ml (¼ pint)	BALSAMIC VINEGAR
150 ml (¼ pint)	TARRAGON OR ROSEMARY VINEGAR

> **INGREDIENTS TIP**
> Replace the allspice, mustard seeds and coriander seeds with 2 teaspoons of pickling spice, if preferred.

Sprinkle the herring fillets with the salt and leave to drain in a colander for 3 hours. Rinse well, dry the fish with kitchen paper, then chill while making the marinade.

To make the marinade, put all the ingredients in a saucepan, bring to the boil and boil for 10 minutes. Remove from the heat and leave to cool.

Spread the filleted side of each piece of fish with mustard. Put the sliced dill pickles and onion on top of the mustard and roll up the fillets, securing them with wooden cocktail sticks.

Put the rolled fillets in a container with an airtight lid and cover with the cold marinade. Seal and store in the refrigerator for 2–7 days. Drain before serving.

VARIATION

Mackerel, salmon, trout or any other oily fish can also be soused in this way.

LADY LLANOVER'S SALT DUCK WITH PICKLED DAMSONS

"Lady Llanover published her cookery book 'The First Principles of Good Cookery' in 1867. In 1991 a facsimile was published. Bobby Freeman asked us to arrange a menu culled from the book for its launch." Taken from Leaves from the Walnut Tree.

FRANCO TARUSCHIO

This recipe was featured in the Gardner Merchant Master Class '95 and appears in the book *Leaves from the Walnut Tree* by Ann and Franco Taruschio.

INGREDIENTS FOR 4 SERVINGS

2 DUCK BREASTS ON THE BONE
COARSE SEA SALT

FOR THE PICKLED DAMSONS

2 litres (3½ pints) DAMSONS
900 g (2 lb) PRESERVING SUGAR
225 ml (8 fl oz) RED WINE VINEGAR
5 cm (2 inch) CINNAMON STICK
3 CLOVES

Weigh the duck breasts and for every 700 g (1½ lb) rub in 50 g (2 oz) sea salt. Put in a deep container, breast side down, and leave in the refrigerator for 3 days, turning over halfway through.

To make the pickled damsons, wash and prick the damsons with a silver fork. Put the sugar and vinegar in a saucepan and heat until the sugar has dissolved. Bring to the boil to make a syrup. Add the damsons and bring back to the boil. Quickly remove the damsons with a slotted spoon and arrange on trays to cool quickly. Add the spices to the syrup and boil for a further 5–10 minutes until thick. Put the fruit into sterilized jars and strain the syrup into the jars while still hot. Cover while still hot and leave to cool. Store in a cool, dark place.

Preheat the oven to 150C/300F/Gas 2. Rinse the salt off the duck breasts. Put in an ovenproof dish and stand the dish in a roasting tin half filled with water. Cover the duck with cold water. Cook, uncovered, for 1½ hours.

Remove the duck from the cooking liquid and leave to cool. Thinly slice and serve with the pickled damsons.

Lady Llanover's Salt Duck with Pickled Damsons

FISH AND SHELLFISH

Salmon and Oats with Cider Sauce

❖

Herb-Crusted Haddock Fillets

❖

Cod and Chips

❖

Roasted Salmon Trout with
Stir-Fried Vegetables

❖

Pan-Fried Cod on a Warm Potato
Vinaigrette

❖

Red Mullet with Caramelized Onions
and Gooseberry Puree

❖

Fried Skate Wings with a Green
Caper Sauce

❖

Dover Sole with Char-Grilled
Bananas

❖

Brill with Asparagus and Tomato
and Herb Dressing

❖

Baked Mackerel Stuffed with Apple,
Pine Nuts and Sultanas

❖

Smoked Fish Pie

❖

Mussels with Cream and Rosemary

❖

Blackened Monkfish with Curried
Aubergine

SALMON AND OATS WITH CIDER SAUCE

A traditional Scottish combination of salmon and oats.

COOKING TIP
When whisking the butter into the cider sauce, use a hand-held electric whisk if you have one, to make the sauce as light as possible.

INGREDIENTS FOR 4 SERVINGS

25 g (1 oz)	PORRIDGE OATS
25 g (1 oz)	FRESH WHITE BREADCRUMBS
	SALT AND FRESHLY GROUND BLACK PEPPER
4 x 100 g (4 oz)	SALMON SUPREMES
2 tablespoons	PLAIN FLOUR
1	EGG, BEATEN
15 g (½ oz)	BUTTER, MELTED

FOR THE CIDER SAUCE

300 ml (½ pint)	STRONG CIDER
150 ml (¼ pint)	DOUBLE CREAM
25 g (1 oz)	BUTTER, DICED
50 g (2 oz)	LEEKS, FINELY SHREDDED

FOR THE GARNISH

50 g (2 oz)	LEEKS, FINELY SHREDDED
	VEGETABLE OIL FOR DEEP FRYING
	DILL SPRIGS

Pre-heat the grill. Mix together the oats and breadcrumbs. Season the salmon and dip the top of each supreme in the flour, then the egg and finally the oat mixture. Put the salmon on a lightly buttered baking sheet, drizzle with melted butter and cook under a moderate grill for 8–10 minutes until golden and cooked through.

Meanwhile, make the cider sauce. Put the cider in a small saucepan and boil rapidly until it has reduced by half. Add the cream, season with salt and simmer for 2 minutes. Whisk in the butter. Add the leeks and heat gently to warm through.

To make the garnish, heat the oil in a deep-fat fryer or large saucepan to 180C/350F. Deep fry the leeks for a few seconds until golden. Drain on kitchen paper.

To serve, spoon the sauce on to a warmed serving plate and put the salmon on top. Garnish with the deep-fried leeks and dill sprigs.

Overleaf:
Salmon and Oats
with Cider Sauce

HERB-CRUSTED HADDOCK FILLETS

This simple recipe gives some style to a versatile but under-rated British fish.

INGREDIENTS FOR 4 SERVINGS

50 g (2 oz)	BUTTER
1 teaspoon	FINELY CHOPPED FRESH PARSLEY
1 teaspoon	FINELY CHOPPED FRESH THYME
1 teaspoon	SNIPPED FRESH CHIVES
6 slices	WHITE BREAD MADE INTO BREADCRUMBS
	SALT AND FRESHLY GROUND BLACK PEPPER
4 x 150 g (5 oz)	HADDOCK FILLETS

Pre-heat the oven to 190C/375F/Gas 5. Melt the butter in a saucepan then add the herbs, breadcrumbs and seasoning. Stir until it forms a dry paste, adding more breadcrumbs if necessary.

Spread the breadcrumb mixture on top of each haddock fillet and put in an ovenproof dish. Bake for 8–10 minutes or until just cooked. Serve with Champ (see page 113) and Runner Beans with Tomato and Herbs (see page 120).

VARIATIONS

This recipe works just as well with turbot, halibut, salmon or cod.

Experiment with your own combinations of herbs in the crust. Try any of the following: Thyme, sage, parsley, dill, chives, mint or coriander. For extra flavour and texture, add finely chopped nuts or grated lemon zest and lemon juice.

COD AND CHIPS

The addition of a few simple ingredients makes all the difference to this great British speciality.

INGREDIENTS TIP
The best potatoes for making chips are King Edward, Maris Piper and Desirée.

COOKING TIP
The batter can be prepared in a food processor or blender but be careful not to overwhisk it.

INGREDIENTS FOR 4 SERVINGS

50 g (2 oz)	PLAIN FLOUR
	SALT AND FRESHLY GROUND BLACK PEPPER
4 x 150 g (5 oz)	COD FILLETS
	VEGETABLE OIL FOR DEEP FRYING
	SPRIGS OF FRESH PARSLEY, TO GARNISH

FOR THE BATTER

175 g (6 oz)	PLAIN FLOUR
200 ml (7 fl oz)	LEMONADE
3 tablespoons	MALT VINEGAR
1½ teaspoons	BAKING POWDER

FOR THE CHIPS

700 g (1½ lb)	POTATOES
100 g (4 oz) each	SWEDES, CARROTS AND CELERY, CUT INTO MATCHSTICKS

FOR THE TARTARE SAUCE

150 ml (¼ pint)	CREME FRAICHE
1 tablespoon	FINELY CHOPPED GHERKINS
1 tablespoon	FINELY CHOPPED CAPERS
1 dessertspoon	FINELY CHOPPED FRESH PARSLEY
1 teaspoon	LEMON JUICE

To make the tartare sauce, mix together all the ingredients. Season and chill until required.

To make the chips, cut the potatoes into 5–10 mm (¼–½ inch) thick slices. Place a few slices on top of each other and cut through to make even-sized chips. Rinse the chips in cold water to remove excess starch and dry well.

Heat the oil in a deep-fat fryer to 150C/300F. Put the chips into a basket and lower into the oil. Deep fry for 5 minutes until soft and just beginning to colour. Remove from the oil and set aside. Increase the oil temperature to 175C/335F. *(Continued on page 56.)*

Cod and Chips

(Continued from page 54.) To make the batter, sift the flour into a bowl then gradually blend in the lemonade and vinegar to make a smooth batter. Sift the baking powder on top.

To prepare the fish, season the flour with salt and pepper and coat the cod, shaking off any excess. Dip the cod fillets into the batter, allowing the excess batter to fall back into the bowl. Put the fish in the hot oil, in batches if necessary, and deep fry for about 7 minutes until golden brown. Remove and drain well on kitchen paper. Keep warm.

Raise the oil temperature to 190C/375F. Add the matchstick vegetables to the oil and fry for about 1 minute until golden. Drain on kitchen paper and keep warm. Return the blanched chips to the hot oil and fry for 5 minutes until golden brown. Drain well, and combine with the other vegetables.

To serve, arrange the chips and deep-fried vegetables on warmed serving plates with the fish. Garnish with parsley sprigs and serve with the tartare sauce.

VARIATIONS

Add some finely chopped herbs to the batter, if you like.

Before coating the fish in flour, marinate it for a few minutes in the juice of ½ lemon and 1 tablespoon of vegetable oil to enhance its flavour and make the fish more moist.

ROASTED SALMON TROUT WITH STIR-FRIED VEGETABLES

The best in home-grown flavours combine beautifully in this recipe.

INGREDIENTS FOR 4 SERVINGS

1 tablespoon	GROUNDNUT OIL
25 g (1 oz)	BUTTER
4 x 150 g (5 oz)	SALMON TROUT FILLETS
25 g (1 oz)	TOASTED PINE NUTS

FOR THE STIR-FRIED VEGETABLES

1 tablespoon	GROUNDNUT OIL
15 g (½ oz)	BUTTER
75 g (3 oz)	LEEKS, SHREDDED
75 g (3 oz)	SHELLED BROAD BEANS, COOKED AND PEELED
75 g (3 oz)	SHELLED PEAS, COOKED
75 g (3 oz)	RUNNER BEANS, BLANCHED AND SHREDDED
1 teaspoon	CHOPPED FRESH ROSEMARY
	SALT AND FRESHLY GROUND BLACK PEPPER

FOR THE BUTTER SAUCE

175 g (6 oz)	BUTTER, DICED
50 ml (2 fl oz)	VEGETABLE STOCK

INGREDIENTS TIP
As fresh peas have such a short season, you could replace them with mange tout or sugar snap peas.

COOKING TIP
Inside the outer skin of a broad bean is a sweeter, more tender bean. To peel broad beans, blanch for 2 minutes, drain, then squeeze the inner bean out of the skin. You will need about 275 g (10 oz) broad beans in their pods and 175 g (6 oz) peas in their pods to give 75 g (3 oz) when shelled.

Pre-heat the oven to 200C/400F/Gas 6. Heat the oil and butter in a frying pan and fry the trout for 2 minutes, turning once.

Transfer the trout to a baking sheet and cook in the oven for about 8 minutes, until just cooked through.

Meanwhile, cook the vegetables. Heat the oil in a large frying pan until lightly smoking. Add the butter and as soon as it starts to foam add the vegetables and rosemary. Stir fry for 3–4 minutes. Season. Remove with a slotted spoon and keep warm.

To make the butter sauce, put the butter and stock in a small saucepan and, over a gentle heat, whisk with a hand-held electric whisk until the sauce begins to simmer and is shiny and smooth.

To serve, put the trout on one side of four warmed serving plates. Arrange the vegetables on the other side, pour a little butter sauce between and sprinkle with a few pine nuts.

PAN-FRIED COD ON A WARM POTATO VINAIGRETTE

A light and refreshing way to serve Britain's favourite fish.

INGREDIENTS FOR 4 SERVINGS

350 g (12 oz)	NEW POTATOES, SCRUBBED
2 tablespoons	OLIVE OIL
	SALT AND FRESHLY GROUND BLACK PEPPER
2 tablespoons	PLAIN FLOUR
4 x 150 g (5 oz)	COD FILLETS, HALVED
25 g (1 oz)	BUTTER
16	CHIVES, TO GARNISH
	PAPRIKA FOR DUSTING

FOR THE VINAIGRETTE

150 ml (¼ pint)	OLIVE OIL
1 tablespoon	SHERRY VINEGAR
1 teaspoon	WHOLEGRAIN MUSTARD
2	TOMATOES, PEELED, SEEDED AND DICED
1 tablespoon	SNIPPED FRESH CHIVES

Cook the potatoes in a saucepan of boiling salted water for 10–15 minutes until just tender. Cut into 5 mm (¼ inch) slices while still hot. Drizzle with a little olive oil, cover and keep warm.

Season the flour with salt and pepper and coat the cod fillets, shaking off any excess. Heat the remaining olive oil and butter in a frying pan. Add the cod, skin side up first, and cook for 6–7 minutes, turning once, until golden and just cooked.

To make the vinaigrette, put the olive oil, vinegar and mustard in a small saucepan and heat gently. Remove from the heat and stir in the tomatoes, chives and seasoning.

To serve, arrange the warm potatoes on four warmed serving plates and spoon over the warm vinaigrette. Sit the cod fillets in the centre of the plate. Dust with paprika and arrange the chives in a trellis pattern on top of the fish.

Pan-Fried Cod on a Warm Potato Vinaigrette

RED MULLET WITH CARAMELIZED ONIONS AND GOOSEBERRY PUREE

The wonderful colours of red mullet and gooseberries make a stunning dish.

SERVING TIP
The slightly bitter taste of a chicory salad goes well with this dish. Onion bread also makes a good accompaniment.

INGREDIENTS FOR 4 SERVINGS

8 x 75 g (3 oz)	RED MULLET FILLETS
	OLIVE OIL FOR BRUSHING

FOR THE CARAMELIZED ONIONS

2 tablespoons	OLIVE OIL
2	LARGE ONIONS, FINELY SLICED
2 teaspoons	DEMERARA SUGAR
1 tablespoon	WHITE WINE VINEGAR

FOR THE GOOSEBERRY PUREE

175 g (6 oz)	GOOSEBERRIES
15 g (½ oz)	BUTTER
50 g (2 oz)	CASTER SUGAR
1 tablespoon	DRY WHITE WINE

To make the caramelized onions, heat the olive oil in a large saucepan and cook the onions, stirring occasionally, for about 20 minutes, until they turn dark brown. Stir in the sugar, remove from the heat, and add the white wine vinegar (stand back as this may create a rush of steam). Stir together and keep warm.

Meanwhile, make the gooseberry purée. Put all the ingredients in a saucepan and simmer for about 10 minutes until the gooseberries are soft. Leave to cool slightly then put in a food processor or blender and process for a few seconds, so that the mixture retains a little texture. Transfer to a clean saucepan and keep warm.

Pre-heat the grill. Brush the red mullet fillets with a little olive oil and grill, turning once, for 5–6 minutes until just cooked.

To serve, spoon a little of the caramelized onions on to four warmed serving plates. Put the red mullet fillets on top and serve the gooseberry purée separately.

FRIED SKATE WINGS WITH A GREEN CAPER SAUCE

This delicious fish is all too often forgotten about. Rediscover it in this simple recipe where it's served with a robust caper sauce.

INGREDIENTS FOR 4 SERVINGS

2 tablespoons	PLAIN FLOUR
	SALT AND FRESHLY GROUND BLACK PEPPER
4 x 225 g (8 oz)	SKATE WINGS
2 tablespoons	VEGETABLE OIL

FOR THE CAPER SAUCE

25 g (1 oz)	BUTTER
2 tablespoons	CAPERS, DRAINED
2	GARLIC CLOVES, FINELY CHOPPED
2 tablespoons	FINELY CHOPPED FRESH BASIL
3 tablespoons	FINELY CHOPPED FRESH PARSLEY
4 tablespoons	LEMON JUICE

INGREDIENTS TIP
Capers are the buds of a bush native to the area around the Mediterranean. They are usually sold in small jars, pickled in vinegar. Their tangy flavour goes well with many fish dishes.

Season the flour with salt and pepper and use to coat the skate wings. Heat the oil in a frying pan until very hot, add the skate and fry for about 5 minutes on each side. To check that the fish is cooked, insert a knife between the bone and flesh, they should part easily. Transfer the skate to warmed serving plates and keep warm.

To make the caper sauce, add the butter to the frying pan and heat gently until melted. Remove the frying pan from the heat. Add the remaining sauce ingredients and swirl around in the pan until just warmed. Season. Pour over the skate and serve.

VARIATION

This sauce will also go well with other flat fish, such as sole or plaice.

DOVER SOLE WITH CHAR-GRILLED BANANAS

This most aristocratic of English fish is best cooked simply.
Char-grilled bananas add an exotic touch.

INGREDIENTS FOR 4 SERVINGS

4	DOVER SOLE, SKINNED
300 ml (½ pint)	FISH STOCK
	VEGETABLE OIL FOR BRUSHING
2	BANANAS
	FRESH HERBS AND LEMON SLICES, TO GARNISH

FOR THE LEMON PARSLEY BUTTER

50 g (2 oz)	BUTTER, SOFTENED
1 teaspoon	LEMON JUICE
2 teaspoons	CHOPPED FRESH PARSLEY

To make the lemon parsley butter, blend the butter with the lemon juice and parsley. Put on to a sheet of baking parchment and form into a roll, about 2.5 cm (1 inch) in diameter. Twist the ends of the baking parchment, to seal. Chill until required.

To prepare the sole, use a sharp knife to cut the fish along the backbone, cutting down to the bone. Run the knife under the flesh on either side of the bone, keeping it attached to the bones at the outer edge. With the palms of the hands, gently roll back the fish on either side of the backbone.

Pre-heat the grill. Put the sole in a single layer in a shallow ovenproof dish (you may have to cook the fish in batches). Add enough hot stock to half cover the fish and grill for 5–6 minutes until the flesh is opaque and firm. Remove with a slotted spoon.

Meanwhile, lightly brush a ridged grill pan with oil and heat until it smokes. Cut the bananas in half, then cut each piece lengthways in half. Grill the flesh of the bananas until browned.

To serve, cut through the backbone of each fish and carefully pull it out. Transfer to warmed serving plates. Add a slice of butter and a piece of banana and garnish with herbs and lemon slices.

Dover Sole with Char-Grilled Bananas

BRILL WITH ASPARAGUS AND TOMATO AND HERB DRESSING

"This simple yet piquant summer dish is served lukewarm." Anton Edelmann.

ANTON EDELMANN

This recipe by Anton Edelmann was featured in the Gardner Merchant Master Class '95 and appears in his book *Anton Edelmann Creative Cuisine*.

INGREDIENTS FOR 4 SERVINGS

16	SMALL ASPARAGUS SPEARS, TRIMMED
4	SKINLESS BRILL FILLETS
	SEA SALT AND FRESHLY GROUND BLACK PEPPER
2 tablespoons	VEGETABLE OIL
	KNOB OF UNSALTED BUTTER
1 tablespoon	WATER
2 dessertspoons	BALSAMIC VINEGAR

FOR THE VINAIGRETTE

150 ml (¼ pint)	OLIVE OIL
3 tablespoons	SHERRY VINEGAR
	SALT AND FRESHLY GROUND BLACK PEPPER
225 g (8 oz)	RIPE BUT FIRM PLUM TOMATOES, PEELED, SEEDED AND DICED
4 tablespoons	MIXED CHOPPED FRESH HERBS, SUCH AS CHIVES, PARSLEY, BASIL AND DILL

Cook the asparagus spears in a saucepan of boiling salted water until just tender but still firm. Drain, then plunge into a bowl of iced water and set aside.

Pre-heat the oven to 200C/400F/Gas 6. Heat a ridged grill pan until very hot. Season the fish with salt and pepper, then brush with the oil. Put the fish on the grill pan and cook for about 25 seconds on each side, rotating the pieces to make a criss-cross pattern from the ridges on the pan.

Transfer the fish to a shallow roasting tin or baking sheet and cover with buttered baking parchment. Cook in the oven for about 8 minutes until the fish is opaque. Test it with the point of a knife – the flesh in the centre should still be slightly translucent.

Put the asparagus in a saucepan with a knob of butter and 1 tablespoon of water. Heat until the water has evaporated and the asparagus is hot. Season. *(Continued on page 66.)*

Brill with Asparagus and Tomato and Herb Dressing

(Continued from page 64.) To make the vinaigrette, whisk together the oil, vinegar and seasoning. Put in a small saucepan and heat gently until luke warm. Stir in the tomatoes and herbs.

To serve, place the fish on warmed serving plates and give it a turn of the peppermill. Pour around the tomato and herb vinaigrette. Arrange the asparagus around the fish and sprinkle everything with balsamic vinegar. Serve immediately.

BAKED MACKEREL STUFFED WITH APPLE, PINE NUTS AND SULTANAS

This deliciously fruity stuffing makes an ideal partner for this rich fish.

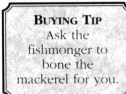

BUYING TIP
Ask the fishmonger to bone the mackerel for you.

INGREDIENTS FOR 4 SERVINGS

4 MEDIUM-SIZED MACKEREL, BONED

FOR THE STUFFING

3 GRANNY SMITH'S APPLES
25 g (1 oz) PINE NUTS, CHOPPED AND TOASTED
3 tablespoons SULTANAS
1 tablespoon SNIPPED FRESH CHIVES
1 tablespoon FRESH BREADCRUMBS
1 tablespoon LEMON JUICE
SALT AND FRESHLY GROUND BLACK PEPPER

Pre-heat the oven to 190C/375F/Gas 5.

To make the stuffing, peel and core the apples and coarsely grate into a bowl. Add the remaining stuffing ingredients and mix thoroughly. Divide the stuffing among the mackerel, packing it tightly into the cavities.

Put the mackerel in an ovenproof dish. Cover and bake for 30 minutes. Serve with the cooking juices spooned over.

SMOKED FISH PIE

This version of fish pie uses smoked cod and haddock to give the dish a real flavour lift.

INGREDIENTS FOR 6–8 SERVINGS

700 g (1½ lb) SMALL DESIREE POTATOES
100 g (4 oz) SMOKED STREAKY BACON, CHOPPED
450 g (1 lb) SMOKED COD
400 g (14 oz) SMOKED HADDOCK
600 ml (1 pint) MILK
75 g (3 oz) BUTTER
3 LEEKS, THINLY SLICED
50 g (2 oz) PLAIN FLOUR
300 ml (½ pint) DRY CIDER
2 tablespoons LEMON JUICE
SALT AND GROUND WHITE PEPPER
100 g (4 oz) COOKED, PEELED PRAWNS
3 tablespoons OLIVE OIL
3 tablespoons GRATED PARMESAN CHEESE

Cook the potatoes in a saucepan of boiling salted water for about 20 minutes until tender. Drain and leave to cool.

Meanwhile, heat a frying pan and dry fry the bacon until crisp. Drain on kitchen paper and set aside. Put the cod and haddock in a large saucepan and cover with the milk. Bring slowly to the boil then simmer for 8–10 minutes until the fish is just cooked. Remove the fish, reserving the milk.

Pre-heat the oven to 190C/375F/Gas 5. Melt the butter in a large saucepan, add the leeks and cook gently for 5 minutes until soft. Add the flour and cook, stirring, for 1 minute. Gradually stir in the reserved milk and the cider to make a smooth sauce. Simmer for 2–3 minutes until thickened. Remove from the heat, add the lemon juice and season.

Remove the skin and any bones from the cod and haddock and flake the flesh. Put the fish in an ovenproof dish with the prawns and bacon. Pour over the sauce.

Slice the potatoes and arrange, overlapping, on top of the fish. Brush with olive oil and sprinkle with Parmesan cheese. Bake for about 30 minutes until the topping is crisp and golden.

MUSSELS WITH CREAM AND ROSEMARY

You'll need a soup spoon and plenty of bread to mop up the delicious sauce with these mussels.

INGREDIENTS FOR 4 SERVINGS

2 kg (4½ lb)	MUSSELS IN THEIR SHELLS
25 g (1 oz)	BUTTER
50 g (2 oz)	SHALLOTS, FINELY CHOPPED
100 ml (4 fl oz)	DRY VERMOUTH
1	SPRIG OF FRESH ROSEMARY
300 ml (½ pint)	FISH STOCK
450 ml (¾ pint)	DOUBLE CREAM
	SALT AND FRESHLY GROUND BLACK PEPPER
	ROSEMARY SPRIGS, TO GARNISH
	CRUSTY BREAD, TO SERVE

Discard any mussels that are open. Scrub the mussels, scrape off any barnacles and use a blunt knife to pull off the beards.

Melt the butter in a large saucepan (that has a tight-fitting lid), add the shallots and cook gently, stirring, for 2 minutes until soft but not coloured.

Add the mussels, vermouth, rosemary and fish stock. Cover and cook for 4–5 minutes until the mussels open. Remove the mussels with a slotted spoon, discarding any that have not opened during cooking. Transfer to warmed serving bowls and keep warm.

Boil the cooking liquid until it has reduced by half, then stir in the cream and boil again until the liquid has reduced by one-third. Season. Remove the rosemary sprig.

To serve, pour the sauce over the mussels, garnish with fresh rosemary sprigs and serve with crusty bread.

Mussels with Cream and Rosemary

BLACKENED MONKFISH WITH CURRIED AUBERGINE

"Blackened fish . . . adapted for the home cook. It is no less delicious, however, even if it is a little bit smokey." Paul and Jeanne Rankin.

PAUL AND JEANNE RANKIN

This recipe by Paul and Jeanne Rankin was featured in the Gardner Merchant Master Class '95 and appears in their book *Hot Food Cool Jazz*.

INGREDIENTS FOR 4 SERVINGS

700 g (1½ lb) BONELESS MONKFISH FILLETS, SKINNED
2 tablespoons LIGHT OLIVE OIL

FOR THE BLACKENING SPICES

1 teaspoon SALT
½ teaspoon each DRIED OREGANO AND THYME
½ teaspoon FRESHLY GROUND BLACK PEPPER
¼ teaspoon GROUND WHITE PEPPER
¼ teaspoon each ONION POWDER, GARLIC POWDER, CAYENNE PEPPER AND PAPRIKA

FOR THE CURRIED AUBERGINE

4 tablespoons LIGHT OLIVE OIL
1 LARGE AUBERGINE, CUT INTO 1 CM (½ INCH) DICE
1 LARGE ONION, THINLY SLICED
1 FRESH GREEN CHILLI, SEEDED AND CHOPPED
1 teaspoon HOT CURRY POWDER
SALT AND FRESHLY GROUND BLACK PEPPER
2 tablespoons CHOPPED FRESH CORIANDER

To make the curried aubergine, heat 3 tablespoons of the oil in a frying pan, add the aubergine and cook for about 6 minutes, until quite soft and browned. Remove and drain on kitchen paper.

Heat the remaining oil in another frying pan and gently cook the onion and chilli for 5 minutes until soft. Add the curry powder and cook for 2 minutes. Add the aubergine and salt and pepper and cook for 2 minutes. Stir in the coriander and keep warm.

Combine the blackening spices. Drizzle the monkfish with half the oil and rub the spices into the fish. Heat a large, heavy frying pan until almost smoking. Add the remaining oil and the monkfish and cook over a high heat for 3 minutes on each side until the seasoning blackens. Serve immediately with curried aubergine.

Blackened Monkfish with Curried Aubergine

MEAT, POULTRY AND GAME

Braised Oxtail with Red Cabbage
❖
Toad in the Hole
❖
Beef Olives with Roasted Vegetables
❖
Cottage Pie
❖
Beef Stew and Dumplings
❖
Steak and Kidney Pudding
❖
Braised Devon Roast
❖
Tenderloin of Welsh Lamb with
Herbs and Grain Mustard
❖
Lancashire Hotpot
❖
Irish Stew
❖
Kidneys in a Mustard Cream Sauce
❖
Glazed Roast Lamb
❖
Boiled Collar of Bacon with
Home-Made Sauerkraut
❖
Pork Chop Rarebit
❖
Sausages and Mash with Onion Gravy
❖
Mustard Roast Gammon with
a Peach Sauce
❖
Honey and Lemon Grilled Chicken
❖
Chicken with Apple and Horseradish
❖
Rabbit with Turnips and Sorrel
❖
Guinea Fowl with Fennel
❖
Duck with Pan-Fried Vegetables and
a Red Onion Sauce
❖
Roasting Meat and Poultry

BRAISED OXTAIL WITH RED CABBAGE

The richness of the oxtail is offset by the tangy red cabbage in this substantial dish.

BUYING TIP
An oxtail weighing about 1.4 kg (3 lb) will be sufficient for 4 servings. Ask your butcher to joint the oxtail for you.

SERVING TIP
Serve with croûtons for a contrasting, crisp accompaniment.

INGREDIENTS FOR 4 SERVINGS

50 g (2 oz) PLAIN FLOUR
SALT AND FRESHLY GROUND BLACK PEPPER
1 OXTAIL, JOINTED
25 g (1 oz) BEEF DRIPPING
2 ONIONS, CHOPPED
2 GARLIC CLOVES, CRUSHED
50 g (2 oz) TOMATO PUREE
600 ml (1 pint) BEEF STOCK
2 BAY LEAVES
FRESH PARSLEY SPRIGS AND BAY LEAVES, TO GARNISH

FOR THE RED CABBAGE

50 g (2 oz) BUTTER
1/2 SMALL RED CABBAGE, SHREDDED
50 g (2 oz) SUGAR
50 ml (2 fl oz) RED WINE VINEGAR
50 ml (2 fl oz) RED WINE
8 CANNED CHESTNUTS, DICED

Pre-heat the oven to 170C/325F/Gas 3. Season the flour with salt and pepper and coat the oxtail pieces in the flour.

Heat the dripping in a flameproof casserole. When hot, add the oxtail and cook until browned all over. Remove with a slotted spoon and set aside. Add the onions and garlic and cook for 5 minutes until soft. Stir in the tomato purée and stock. Return the oxtail to the casserole, add the bay leaves and bring to the boil, stirring. Cover and cook in the oven for 2 hours until tender.

Meanwhile, make the red cabbage. Melt the butter in a casserole, add the cabbage and cook for 5 minutes. Stir in the sugar, vinegar, wine and seasoning, cover and bake for 40 minutes.

Garnish the oxtail with parsley and bay leaves and serve with the red cabbage, topped with a liberal sprinkling of diced chestnuts.

Overleaf: Braised Oxtail with Red Cabbage

TOAD IN THE HOLE

An unusual version of this old favourite, made with a mixture of meats instead of sausages.

INGREDIENTS FOR 4 SERVINGS

150 g (5 oz) STREAKY BACON RASHERS
50 ml (2 fl oz) VEGETABLE OIL
175 g (6 oz) SIRLOIN STEAK, DICED
175 g (6 oz) LAMB'S KIDNEYS, CORED AND DICED
ONION GRAVY (SEE PAGE 95), TO SERVE

FOR THE BATTER

175 g (6 oz) PLAIN FLOUR
SALT AND FRESHLY GROUND BLACK PEPPER
450 ml (¾ pint) MILK
3 EGGS

> **COOKING TIP**
> The batter can be prepared in a food processor or blender, but be careful not to over-beat it otherwise too much air will be incorporated into the mix.

Pre-heat the oven to 220C/425F/Gas 7. Roll up the bacon rashers. Heat the oil in a frying pan and gently fry the steak, kidneys and bacon rolls until browned. Remove with a slotted spoon and set aside, reserving the oil.

To make the batter, sift the flour into a bowl and season. Make a well in the centre of the flour, break in the eggs and pour in half of the milk. Gradually whisk the flour into the egg and milk to make a smooth batter. Whisk in the remaining milk.

Pour the reserved cooking oil into an ovenproof dish and put in the oven. When the oil is smoking, add half the batter and return the dish to the oven for about 10 minutes, until just set.

Remove the dish from the oven and arrange the steak, kidneys and bacon on top of the set batter. Pour over the remaining batter. Bake for about 20 minutes, until the batter is well risen. Serve immediately with onion gravy.

VARIATIONS

For a more traditional version, use sausages instead of or in addition to the meats, adjusting the quantities accordingly.

Add finely chopped herbs to the batter mix, but be careful if using sausages that are already flavoured with herbs.

Beef Olives with Roasted Vegetables

*Rolls of steak slowly cooked with an aromatic stuffing
and rich sauce, with their own accompaniment
of roasted vegetables.*

Ingredients for 4 servings

8 x 75 g (3 oz)	THIN SLICES BRAISING STEAK
2 tablespoons	VEGETABLE OIL
100 g (4 oz) each	CELERY, ONION AND CARROT, FINELY DICED
50 g (2 oz)	PLAIN FLOUR
1 dessertspoon	TOMATO PUREE
450 ml (¾ pint)	RICH BEEF STOCK
	PINCH OF GROUND MACE
	CHOPPED FRESH PARSLEY, TO GARNISH

For the stuffing

100 g (4 oz)	MINCED BEEF
50 g (2 oz)	STREAKY BACON, FINELY CHOPPED
40 g (1½ oz)	FRESH WHITE BREADCRUMBS
	GRATED ZEST OF 1 LEMON
1 teaspoon	FINELY CHOPPED FRESH THYME
1 teaspoon	FINELY CHOPPED FRESH MARJORAM
1 teaspoon	SNIPPED FRESH CHIVES
	SALT AND FRESHLY GROUND BLACK PEPPER
1	EGG, BEATEN

For the roasted vegetables

2 tablespoons	VEGETABLE OIL
25 g (1 oz)	SUGAR
8	SHALLOTS
8	CARROTS, HALVED AND TURNED
8	PARSNIPS, SLICED

Pre-heat the oven to 170C/325F/Gas 3. To make the stuffing, mix together all the ingredients in a bowl. Trim the steaks and lightly flatten. Put a spoonful of stuffing in the centre of each steak, roll up and secure with wooden cocktail sticks. *(Continued on page 78.)*

Beef Olives with Roasted Vegetables

(Continued from page 76.) Heat the oil in a frying pan, add the beef olives and cook briefly until lightly browned all over. Remove with a slotted spoon and place in an ovenproof dish. Add the celery, onion and carrot to the pan and cook until browned. Stir in the flour and the tomato purée and cook, stirring, for 1 minute. Gradually add the stock, stirring until thickened. Add the mace and seasoning and pour the sauce over the beef olives. Cover and cook in the oven for 1 hour.

To make the roasted vegetables, increase the oven temperature to 220C/425F/Gas 7 20 minutes before the end of the beef olives' cooking time. Heat the oil and sugar in a roasting tin. When the oil is producing a light haze, add the vegetables and turn to coat in the oil. Roast for 20–30 minutes, basting occasionally, until tender.

To serve, remove the beef olives from the casserole with a slotted spoon. Arrange six in the centre of a serving dish. Slice the remaining two beef olives and arrange on top. Pour over a little sauce and arrange the vegetables around the olives. Serve the remaining sauce separately.

VARIATIONS

If you have time, marinating the steaks will reduce the cooking time and enhance the flavour of the beef. Combine 150 ml (¼ pint) red wine, 1 teaspoon chopped fresh basil, 2 crushed garlic cloves, 2 tablespoons red wine vinegar, 50 ml (2 fl oz) vegetable oil and 50 g (2 oz) tomato purée. Add the steaks and leave to marinate for 3 hours. Remove from the marinade, reserving the marinade, dry the steaks on kitchen paper and continue as above, replacing 150 ml (¼ pint) of the stock with the marinade.

For a richer version of this recipe, try Beef Olives au Poivre. Proceed as above. When the olives are cooked, remove from the sauce and boil the sauce until reduced to 300 ml (½ pint). Strain the sauce and add 75 ml (3 fl oz) double cream, 50 g (2 oz) green peppercorns and 25 ml (1 fl oz) brandy. Heat through and serve with the beef olives as above.

COTTAGE PIE

A recipe with a twist – the potato is combined with swede to give a lovely golden-coloured topping.

INGREDIENTS FOR 4 SERVINGS

1 tablespoon	VEGETABLE OIL
4	SHALLOTS, FINELY DICED
1	GARLIC CLOVE, CRUSHED
100 g (4 oz)	CARROT, DICED
450 g (1 lb)	MINCED BEEF
25 g (1 oz)	PLAIN FLOUR
2 tablespoons	TOMATO PUREE
4	TOMATOES, PEELED, SEEDED AND CHOPPED
225 ml (8 fl oz)	BEEF STOCK
	SALT AND FRESHLY GROUND BLACK PEPPER

FOR THE TOPPING

275 g (10 oz)	SWEDE, CUT INTO CHUNKS
1 teaspoon	CREAMED HORSERADISH
275 g (10 oz)	POTATOES, CUT INTO CHUNKS
25 g (1 oz)	BUTTER
2 tablespoons	WARMED MILK

Heat the oil in a frying pan, add the shallots, garlic and carrot and cook gently for 3 minutes. Add the beef and cook, stirring, until browned. Sprinkle on the flour and cook, stirring, for 3 minutes.

Add the tomato purée, chopped tomatoes, stock and seasoning. Bring to the boil and simmer gently for 30 minutes, stirring occasionally. Pre-heat the oven to 180C/350F/Gas 4.

Meanwhile, make the topping. Cook the swede in boiling salted water for 10–15 minutes until soft. Drain and mash with the creamed horseradish. Cook the potatoes in boiling salted water for 10–15 minutes until soft. Drain and mash with the butter and warmed milk. Mix together the swede and potato.

Season the meat mixture to taste and transfer to an ovenproof dish. Spread or pipe the potato mixture on top of the meat. Bake for 30 minutes until the topping is golden brown.

BEEF STEW AND DUMPLINGS

A simple, hearty dish – just what's needed on a cold winter's day.

INGREDIENTS FOR 4 SERVINGS

SALT AND FRESHLY GROUND BLACK PEPPER
25 g (1 oz) PLAIN FLOUR
450 g (1 lb) BRAISING STEAK, DICED
25 g (1 oz) LARD
1 ONION, FINELY DICED
50 g (2 oz) CARROTS, DICED
50 g (2 oz) LEEK, SLICED
50 g (2 oz) CELERY, DICED
300 ml (½ pint) STOUT
600 ml (1 pint) BEEF STOCK
25 g (1 oz) TOMATO PUREE
100 g (4 oz) MUSHROOMS, QUARTERED
1 BAY LEAF

FOR THE DUMPLINGS

225 g (8 oz) PLAIN FLOUR
1 teaspoon BAKING POWDER
1 teaspoon SALT
100 g (4 oz) SHREDDED BEEF SUET
2 LARGE SAGE LEAVES, FINELY CHOPPED
75 ml (3 fl oz) COLD CHICKEN STOCK

Pre-heat the oven to 170C/325F/Gas 3. Season the flour and use to coat the meat. Heat the lard in an ovenproof casserole. Add the meat and cook until browned. Remove with a slotted spoon.

Add the onion, carrots, leek and celery and cook for 7 minutes until lightly browned. Stir in the remaining flour. Add the stout and stock, stirring well. Bring to the boil. Stir in the tomato purée, meat, mushrooms and bay leaf and cook for 2 hours until tender.

To make the dumplings, sift the flour, baking powder and salt into a bowl. Stir in the suet and sage. Add enough stock to form a smooth dough. Divide the dough into twelve and lightly roll into balls. Add to the stew 15 minutes before the end of the cooking time. Cover and cook until the dumplings are risen.

Beef Stew and Dumplings

STEAK AND KIDNEY PUDDING

A truly British classic – a richly flavoured meat filling with a light suet crust.

COOKING TIP
For extra flavour, marinate the meat in the wine for 24 hours. Drain the meat, reserving the wine, and pat dry on kitchen paper before browning. Add the wine as in the recipe.

INGREDIENTS FOR 4–6 SERVINGS

25 g (1 oz)	PLAIN FLOUR
	SALT AND FRESHLY GROUND BLACK PEPPER
450 g (1 lb)	BRAISING STEAK, DICED
100 g (4 oz)	PIG'S KIDNEY, CORED AND DICED
2 tablespoons	VEGETABLE OIL
100 g (4 oz)	ONION, CHOPPED
1	SPRIG OF THYME
1	BAY LEAF
300 ml (½ pint)	BEEF STOCK
300 ml (½ pint)	RED WINE

FOR THE SUET PASTRY

350 g (12 oz)	SELF-RAISING FLOUR
175 g (6 oz)	BEEF SUET
200 ml (7 fl oz)	WATER

Season the flour with salt and pepper and use to coat the steak and kidney. Heat the oil in a flameproof casserole, add the steak, kidney and onion and cook, stirring, for 10 minutes. Add the thyme, bay leaf, stock and wine. Bring to the boil, stirring constantly. Cover and simmer for 1 hour. Leave to cool.

To make the suet pastry, sift the flour into a bowl and stir in the suet and seasoning. Add enough water to form a smooth dough. Roll out three-quarters of the pastry and use to line a 1.1 litre (2 pint) pudding basin.

Spoon the meat mixture into the basin. Roll out the remaining pastry to form a lid. Dampen the edge of the pastry with a little water and put the lid on top. Seal the edges. Cover with a piece of pleated baking parchment then a piece of pleated foil and secure by tying string beneath the rim.

Put into a large saucepan and pour in enough boiling water to come halfway up the sides of the basin. Cover and steam for 2 hours, topping up with boiling water as necessary. Turn out on to a warmed serving plate or serve straight from the basin.

VARIATIONS

The suet pastry can be flavoured with grated lemon zest, chopped fresh marjoram, ground mace or grated nutmeg.

Steak and Kidney Pie: Cook the steak and kidney for a total of 2 hours. Put into a pie dish and top with 175 g (6 oz) shortcrust or puff pastry. Brush the pastry with beaten egg and make a small slit in the top. Bake at 220C/425F/Gas 7 for 20 minutes. Reduce the oven temperature to 180C/350F/Gas 4 and cook for 20 minutes.

BRAISED DEVON ROAST

A dish combining Britain's favourite ingredients – beef and beer.

INGREDIENTS FOR 4–6 SERVINGS

15 g (½ oz)	BEEF DRIPPING
900 g (2 lb)	SILVERSIDE OF BEEF
75 g (3 oz)	ONIONS, SLICED
1	GARLIC CLOVE, FINELY CHOPPED
300 ml (½ pint)	STRONG BITTER
300 ml (½ pint)	BEEF STOCK
50 g (2 oz)	TOMATO PUREE
1 tablespoon	CHOPPED FRESH THYME
1 tablespoon	CHOPPED FRESH PARSLEY
	SALT AND FRESHLY GROUND BLACK PEPPER
350 g (12 oz)	FIELD MUSHROOMS, DICED

Pre-heat the oven to 200C/400F/Gas 6. Heat the dripping in a flameproof casserole, add the beef and cook, turning, until browned all over. Remove the meat and set aside.

Reduce the heat, add the onions and garlic and cook, stirring, for 5 minutes until soft. Stir in the beer and stock and bring to the boil. Add the tomato purée, thyme, parsley and seasoning. Return the beef to the pan, surround it with the mushrooms, cover and cook in the oven for 2 hours until the meat is tender.

Remove the meat, wrap in foil and keep warm. Skim any fat from the sauce then simmer for 10 minutes until reduced by half.

To serve, slice the beef and arrange on a serving plate. Spoon over the sauce and mushrooms.

TENDERLOIN OF WELSH LAMB WITH HERBS AND GRAIN MUSTARD

"It is vital that food is handled carefully or it will be spoiled, and for the very best results it must then be prepared sensitively and cooked with love." Taken from The Essential Mosimann.

ANTON MOSIMANN

This recipe by Anton Mosimann was featured in the Gardner Merchant Master Class '95 and appears in his book *The Essential Mosimann.*

INGREDIENTS FOR 4 SERVINGS

4 x 115 g (4½ oz) NOISETTES OF WELSH LAMB, CUT FROM THE LOIN
SALT AND FRESHLY GROUND BLACK PEPPER
225 g (8 oz) PEELED SLICED VEGETABLES (A MIXTURE OF CARROTS, RED ONIONS AND BABY LEEKS)
2 teaspoons each DIJON AND WHOLEGRAIN MUSTARD
4 tablespoons FINELY SNIPPED FRESH CHIVES (OR A MIXTURE OF CHOPPED PARSLEY, CHIVES, BASIL AND TARRAGON)

FOR THE SAUCE

200 ml (7 fl oz) BROWN LAMB STOCK
1 teaspoon WHOLEGRAIN MUSTARD

FOR THE MARINADE

1 GARLIC CLOVE, CHOPPED
1 SPRIG OF THYME
1 SPRIG OF ROSEMARY
2 tablespoons OLIVE OIL

Trim the noisettes, cutting off all the fat. Put the marinade ingredients in a shallow dish, add the lamb and marinate for at least 2 hours.

Pre-heat the grill. Remove the lamb from the marinade, season and grill or char-grill for 2–3 minutes on each side, until browned on the outside but still pink in the centre.

Meanwhile, to make the sauce, boil the lamb stock until reduced by half. Add the mustard and heat gently.

Steam the vegetables or stir fry in a little butter and season well. Mix together the Dijon and wholegrain mustards and brush over one side of each piece of lamb. Dip the mustard-coated side of the lamb noisettes into the herbs, shaking off any surplus.

To serve, divide the vegetables among four warmed serving plates, spoon over a little of the sauce and top with the lamb.

Tenderloin of Welsh Lamb with Herbs and Grain Mustard

LANCASHIRE HOTPOT

A less traditional version of this famous dish, but one that enhances the flavours of the ingredients.

INGREDIENTS FOR 4–6 SERVINGS

2 tablespoons	VEGETABLE OIL
450 g (1 lb)	SHOULDER OF LAMB, CUBED
	SALT AND FRESHLY GROUND BLACK PEPPER
25 g (1 oz)	SUGAR
1	LARGE ONION, SLICED
175 g (6 oz)	LAMB'S KIDNEYS, CORED AND DICED
300 ml (½ pint)	LAMB STOCK
1 teaspoon	CHOPPED FRESH ROSEMARY
1 teaspoon	CHOPPED FRESH THYME
450 g (1 lb)	POTATOES, THICKLY SLICED
25 g (1 oz)	BUTTER, MELTED

Pre-heat the oven to 180C/350F/Gas 4. Heat the oil in a frying pan, add the lamb and cook, stirring, until browned all over. Season well and stir in the sugar. Remove the lamb with a slotted spoon and put in a deep ovenproof dish. Arrange the onion slices on top.

Return the pan to the heat, add the kidneys and cook, stirring, until lightly browned. Arrange the kidneys on top of the meat. Add the stock and herbs to the frying pan and heat, stirring, to deglaze the pan. Pour the stock over the meat and kidneys.

Neatly arrange the potatoes over the meat and kidneys. Cover the dish with a lid or piece of foil and bake for 2 hours.

Increase the oven temperature to 220C/425F/Gas 7. Remove the lid or foil and brush the potatoes with the melted butter. Return to the oven and cook for 15 minutes until the potatoes are lightly browned and crisp.

VARIATIONS

In the 17th century, oysters were often added to a hotpot because they were so cheap. Add 6 oysters when layering the ingredients.

Replace the potato topping with a garlic crust. Cut half a French stick into 1 cm (½ inch) slices. Stir 2 crushed garlic cloves into 150 g (5 oz) melted butter. Dip the bread into the butter. Arrange on top of the meat 30 minutes before the end of cooking time.

Lancashire Hotpot

IRISH STEW

This one-pot meal requires long, slow cooking to develop the flavours and ensure the lamb is meltingly tender.

INGREDIENTS FOR 4 SERVINGS

550 g (1¼ lb) SHOULDER OF LAMB, DICED
700 g (1½ lb) POTATOES
450 g (1 lb) ONIONS, CUT INTO CHUNKS
SALT AND FRESHLY GROUND BLACK PEPPER
1 SPRIG OF THYME, FINELY CHOPPED
1 SPRIG OF PARSLEY, FINELY CHOPPED
1 litre (1¾ pints) LAMB STOCK
75 g (3 oz) PEARL BARLEY

Pre-heat the oven to 180C/350F/Gas 4. Trim the meat of any excess fat and skin. Slice half of the potatoes and arrange in the base of an ovenproof dish. Add the lamb and onions and season well. Sprinkle over the thyme and parsley. Cut the remaining potatoes into fairly large dice and arrange evenly over the meat.

Put the stock in a saucepan and bring to the boil. Add the pearl barley, stir together and pour into the casserole until the liquid is level with the meat.

Cover with a lid or piece of foil and bake for 2–2½ hours. Check after 1 hour and add a little extra stock or water if necessary.

VARIATION

Slice all the potato and arrange in the dish with alternate layers of meat and onions, but remember to add the pearl barley and stock before the final layer of potato.

KIDNEYS IN A MUSTARD CREAM SAUCE

Tender lamb's kidneys in a richly flavoured sauce.

INGREDIENTS FOR 4 SERVINGS

700 g (1½ lb)	LAMB'S KIDNEYS
2 tablespoons	VEGETABLE OIL
25 g (1 oz)	BUTTER
½	ONION, FINELY CHOPPED
1 tablespoon	DRY SHERRY
150 ml (¼ pint)	CHICKEN STOCK
300 ml (½ pint)	DOUBLE CREAM
2 tablespoons	SNIPPED FRESH CHIVES
2 tablespoons	WHOLEGRAIN MUSTARD
	SALT AND GROUND WHITE PEPPER
50 g (2 oz)	OYSTER MUSHROOMS, SLICED

Cut the kidneys in half, remove the core and cut in half again. Heat the oil and half the butter in a frying pan, add the kidneys and cook for 3 minutes, turning, until lightly browned. Remove with a slotted spoon and set aside.

Add the onions to the pan and cook for 3 minutes until soft but not coloured. Add the sherry and chicken stock. Bring to the boil and simmer until almost all of the liquid has evaporated.

Stir in the cream, three-quarters of the chives and the mustard. Heat gently, stirring, until the sauce has thickened. Season, then return the kidneys to the pan and cook for 4–5 minutes.

Meanwhile, melt the remaining butter in a frying pan, add the mushrooms and cook until lightly browned.

To serve, arrange the kidneys on warmed serving plates, place the fried mushrooms on top and spoon over the sauce. Sprinkle with the remaining chives and serve.

VARIATION
This recipe works just as well with strips of lamb's liver instead of the kidneys.

GLAZED ROAST LAMB

For a special occasion or Sunday lunch, serve this succulent leg of lamb, coated in a sticky, fruity glaze.

> **COOKING TIP**
> To make it easier to slice the potatoes, insert a skewer through the lower half of the potato, and slice through the potato – the skewer will stop you cutting all the way through. Remove the skewer before cooking.

INGREDIENTS FOR 4 SERVINGS

1	LEG OF LAMB
225 g (8 oz)	REDCURRANT JELLY
100 g (4 oz)	MINT JELLY
	MINT SPRIGS, TO GARNISH

FOR THE FANTAIL POTATOES

12	MEDIUM-SIZED POTATOES
	OIL FOR BRUSHING
	SALT AND FRESHLY GROUND BLACK PEPPER

Pre-heat the oven to 220C/425F/Gas 7. Weigh the lamb and calculate the cooking time, allowing 25 minutes per 450 g (1 lb) plus 25 minutes. Use a sharp knife to score the skin of the lamb.

Put the redcurrant jelly and mint jelly in a small saucepan and heat until melted and combined. Brush all over the lamb. Put the lamb in a roasting tin and roast for 30 minutes.

Reduce the oven temperature to 180C/350F/Gas 4 and roast the lamb for the remainder of the calculated cooking time, basting every 30 minutes.

Meanwhile, make the fantail potatoes. Trim the potatoes into neat barrel shapes. Slice them at 5 mm (¼ inch) intervals, being careful not to cut all the way through. Put in a roasting tin and brush with the oil. Season with salt and pepper and cook for 30 minutes, brushing occasionally with more oil.

Remove the lamb from the oven and let stand for 10 minutes before carving. Serve with the fantail potatoes.

Glazed Roast Lamb with Fantail Potatoes

BOILED COLLAR OF BACON WITH HOME-MADE SAUERKRAUT

"The beauty of boiling meat is that it creates its own stock as it cooks, which then becomes the base for the sauce." Gary Rhodes.

This recipe by Gary Rhodes was featured in the Gardner Merchant Master Class '95 and appears in his book *More Rhodes Around Britain.*

INGREDIENTS FOR 4–6 SERVINGS

900 g–1.4 kg (2–3 lb)	BACON COLLAR, BONED, SKINNED, ROLLED AND TIED
1	ONION, ROUGHLY CHOPPED
2	CARROTS, ROUGHLY CHOPPED
2	CELERY STICKS, ROUGHLY CHOPPED
1	BAY LEAF
1–1.7 litres (2–3 pints)	CHICKEN STOCK OR WATER
150 ml (¼ pint)	DOUBLE CREAM
25 g (1 oz)	UNSALTED BUTTER
1–2 teaspoons	MUSTARD SEEDS
	SALT AND GROUND WHITE PEPPER
1 quantity	HOME-MADE SAUERKRAUT (SEE PAGE 114), TO SERVE

Soak the bacon in cold water for 24 hours to remove excess salt.

Drain the bacon and rinse. Put in a saucepan with the vegetables and bay leaf. Cover with the stock or water. Bring to a simmer and simmer for 1–1½ hours. Leave to rest in the cooking liquor for 20 minutes.

Drain 600 ml (1 pint) of the cooking liquor into a saucepan. Bring to the boil and boil until reduced by half. Add the cream to the reduced stock and cook for 10 minutes. Whisk in the butter and mustard seeds to taste. Season.

To serve, carve the bacon, allowing two slices per person. Spoon the Sauerkraut on to warmed serving plates, arrange the bacon at the side and spoon around the sauce.

Boiled Collar of Bacon with Home-Made Sauerkraut

PORK CHOP RAREBIT

An unusual, meaty version of Welsh rarebit.

COOKING TIP
Be careful not to
overcook the
rarebit mixture or
the cheese will
become stringy.

INGREDIENTS FOR 4 SERVINGS

4 x 175 g (6 oz) BONELESS PORK CHOPS

FOR THE RAREBIT

7.5 g (¼ oz) BUTTER
100 g (4 oz) MATURE CHEDDAR CHEESE, GRATED
2 tablespoons BEER
½ teaspoon ENGLISH MUSTARD
½ teaspoon WORCESTERSHIRE SAUCE
SALT AND FRESHLY GROUND BLACK PEPPER

To make the rarebit, melt the butter in a saucepan, add the cheese and cook gently, stirring, until melted. Add the beer, mustard, Worcestershire sauce and seasoning and stir until well blended. Remove from the heat and leave to cool.

Pre-heat the grill. Grill the pork chops under a moderate heat for about 10 minutes on each side until cooked through. Leave to cool slightly. Spread the chops with a thick layer of the rarebit mixture. Return them to the grill and grill until the cheese bubbles and begins to brown.

Serve with grilled apple rings, Wilted Spinach with Garlic (see page 123) and Pan-Fried Potatoes (see page 118).

SAUSAGES AND MASH WITH ONION GRAVY

Use home-made sausages to turn this classic into a high-class dish.

INGREDIENTS FOR 4 SERVINGS

25 g (1 oz)	BEEF DRIPPING
8	PORK AND LEEK SAUSAGES (SEE PAGE 14)

FOR THE ONION GRAVY

2 teaspoons	VEGETABLE OIL
4	ONIONS, FINELY SLICED
2 teaspoons	RINDLESS MARMALADE
600 ml (1 pint)	BEEF STOCK
	SALT AND FRESHLY GROUND BLACK PEPPER

FOR THE MASHED POTATOES

700 g (1½ lb)	POTATOES, CUT INTO CHUNKS
25 g (1 oz)	BUTTER, MELTED
2 tablespoons	WARMED MILK

FOR THE GARNISH

	VEGETABLE OIL FOR DEEP FRYING
2	ONIONS, FINELY SLICED INTO RINGS

To make the gravy, heat the vegetable oil in a saucepan. Add the onions and cook gently, stirring occasionally, for 20–30 minutes, until they turn very brown and caramelize. Stir in the marmalade and the stock. Heat through, season and keep warm.

Meanwhile, heat the dripping in a frying pan and fry the sausages for 15–20 minutes. Cook the potatoes in boiling salted water for 20 minutes until tender. Drain, return to the pan and heat for a few seconds to dry them. Mash until smooth. Beat in the melted butter, warmed milk and seasoning. Keep warm.

To make the garnish, heat the oil in a deep-fat fryer or large saucepan to 190C/375F. Fry the onion rings until crisp and golden.

To serve, spoon the mashed potatoes on to warmed serving plates. Put the sausages on the plates, spoon the onion gravy around and arrange the deep-fried onions on top.

MUSTARD ROAST GAMMON WITH A PEACH SAUCE

With its nutty, tangy crust and fruity peach sauce this roast gammon can grace any special occasion (illustrated on pages 178–9).

INGREDIENTS FOR 8–10 SERVINGS

1.8 kg (4 lb)	GAMMON JOINT
1	ONION
3	CLOVES
1	BAY LEAF
6	BLACK PEPPERCORNS
225 ml (8 fl oz)	DRY WHITE WINE

FOR THE MUSTARD CRUST

1 tablespoon	WHOLEGRAIN MUSTARD
50 g (2 oz)	CHOPPED MIXED NUTS
2 tablespoons	CLEAR HONEY
1 tablespoon	SESAME SEEDS

FOR THE PEACH SAUCE

25 g (1 oz)	BUTTER
$\frac{1}{4}$ teaspoon	GROUND CLOVES
$\frac{1}{4}$ teaspoon	GROUND ALLSPICE
1 tablespoon	SOFT BROWN SUGAR
4 tablespoons	BRANDY
6	RIPE PEACHES, PEELED AND SLICED

Soak the gammon in plenty of cold water for at least 3 hours. Drain the gammon and discard the water. Put the joint in a large saucepan and cover with cold water. Stud the onion with the cloves and add to the pan with the bay leaf, peppercorns and wine. Bring to the boil, cover and simmer for 1 hour. Leave to cool, still in the water.

Pre-heat the oven to 200C/400F/Gas 6. To make the mustard crust, mix together all the ingredients. With a sharp knife, remove the rind from the gammon and score the fat into diamond shapes. Spread over the mustard mixture, put the gammon in a roasting tin and roast for 45 minutes, basting 3 or 4 times during cooking.

Meanwhile, make the peach sauce. Melt the butter in a

saucepan. Add the ground cloves, allspice and sugar and stir well. Add the brandy and bring to the boil. Add the peaches, cover and simmer, stirring occasionally, for about 7 minutes, until tender.

Reserve a few whole peach slices. Put the remainder in a food processor or blender with the cooking juices and process until smooth. Return to the pan with the whole slices and warm through.

Serve the gammon warm or cold, with the peach sauce.

HONEY AND LEMON
GRILLED CHICKEN

Leave this sweet and sour chicken to marinate overnight, then when you're ready to eat, it's cooked in minutes.

INGREDIENTS FOR 4 SERVINGS

4 x 175 g (6 oz) BONELESS CHICKEN BREASTS
WILTED SPINACH WITH GARLIC, TO SERVE
(SEE PAGE 123)

FOR THE MARINADE

JUICE OF 1 ORANGE
JUICE OF 1 LEMON
FEW SPRIGS OF THYME
2 tablespoons CLEAR HONEY
1 GARLIC CLOVE, CRUSHED
SALT AND FRESHLY GROUND BLACK PEPPER

> **COOKING TIP**
> This would make a great dish for a barbecue.

Put the chicken breasts in a single layer in a dish just large enough to accommodate them. To make the marinade, mix together all the ingredients and pour over the chicken. Turn to coat in the marinade, cover and marinate overnight in the refrigerator.

Pre-heat the grill. Remove the chicken from the marinade and put on a grill rack with a tray beneath. Spoon the marinade over the chicken. Cook under a moderate grill for 15 minutes, basting with the marinade every 5 minutes.

To serve, place the spinach on warmed serving plates, place a chicken breast on top and spoon over the cooking juices.

CHICKEN WITH APPLE AND HORSERADISH

A traditional roast with a twist – an unusual new sauce and an accompaniment of crispy fried parsnips.

INGREDIENTS FOR 4 SERVINGS

25 g (1 oz) BUTTER
1.6 kg (3½ lb) ROASTING CHICKEN

FOR THE APPLE SAUCE

2 COOKING APPLES, PEELED, CORED AND CHOPPED
JUICE OF ¼ LEMON
50 ml (2 fl oz) WATER
1 tablespoon CREAMED HORSERADISH
150 ml (¼ pint) RICH GRAVY (OPTIONAL)
2 tablespoons DOUBLE CREAM

FOR THE PARSNIP CHIPS

2 PARSNIPS
VEGETABLE OIL FOR DEEP FRYING
SALT

Pre-heat the oven to 200C/400F/Gas 6. Melt the butter in a roasting tin, add the chicken and baste with the butter. Roast for about 1½ hours, basting occasionally with the butter and juices. Remove from the oven and let stand for 10 minutes.

Meanwhile, make the apple sauce. Put the apples, lemon juice and water in a saucepan and cook gently for 10 minutes, until soft. Remove the pan from the heat and beat to a purée. Stir in the horseradish, gravy, if using, and cream. Heat gently.

To make the parsnip chips, trim and peel the parsnips. Use a vegetable peeler to cut the parsnips lengthways into thin ribbons. Heat the oil in a deep-fat fryer or large saucepan to 190C/375F. Deep fry the parsnips until golden and crisp. Drain on kitchen paper and sprinkle with salt.

To serve, carve the chicken and arrange the meat on serving plates with the parsnip chips. Spoon a little of the sauce on to the plates and serve the remainder separately.

Chicken with Apple and Horseradish, served with courgettes and quenelles of puréed carrot and swede.

Rabbit with Turnips and Sorrel

Rediscover this delicious lean meat, delicately flavoured with sorrel and baby turnips.

INGREDIENTS TIP
If turnips with their leaves are not available, simply use trimmed turnips.

INGREDIENTS FOR 4 SERVINGS

25 g (1 oz)	PLAIN FLOUR
	SALT AND FRESHLY GROUND BLACK PEPPER
4 x 175 g (6 oz)	RABBIT PORTIONS (LEG OR LOIN)
75 g (3 oz)	BUTTER
12	SMALL TURNIPS WITH THEIR LEAVES
40 g (1½ oz)	SORREL, SHREDDED
225 g (8 oz)	ONION, CHOPPED
900 ml (1½ pints)	HOT CHICKEN STOCK
2 teaspoons	SUGAR

Pre-heat the oven to 170C/325F/Gas 3. Season the flour with salt and pepper and use to coat the rabbit portions.

Melt the butter in a flameproof casserole. Add the rabbit and cook until lightly browned all over. Remove with a slotted spoon and set aside.

Remove the leaves from the turnips, add to the casserole with the sorrel, turnips and onion and cook for 5 minutes. Stir in the stock and sugar.

Return the rabbit to the casserole. Bring to the boil, cover and cook in the oven for 1½ hours.

To serve, arrange the turnip and sorrel leaves on a serving dish. Arrange the rabbit and turnips on top and spoon over the sauce.

GUINEA FOWL WITH FENNEL

Tender guinea fowl, flavoured with a garlic and fennel marinade
and topped with a crisp poppy seed crust.

INGREDIENTS FOR 4 SERVINGS

1.1 kg (2½ lb) GUINEA FOWL, JOINTED
75 g (3 oz) WHOLEMEAL BREADCRUMBS
15 g (½ oz) POPPY SEEDS
300 ml (½ pint) BEEF JUS (SEE PAGE 33)

FOR THE MARINADE

50 ml (2 fl oz) OLIVE OIL
JUICE OF 1 LEMON
1 GARLIC CLOVE, CRUSHED
50 g (2 oz) FENNEL, FINELY CHOPPED
SALT AND FRESHLY GROUND BLACK PEPPER

> **COOKING TIP**
> If you haven't time to make your own beef jus, simply use beef stock and a little cornflour to make a gravy.

To make the marinade, combine the oil, lemon juice, garlic, fennel and seasoning. Add the guinea fowl and turn to coat in the marinade. Cover and chill for at least 4 hours, turning occasionally.

Pre-heat the oven to 200C/400F/Gas 6. Remove the guinea fowl from the marinade, reserving the marinade, and put in a roasting tin. Cover and cook in the oven for 25 minutes.

Meanwhile, stir the breadcrumbs and poppy seeds into the remaining marinade. Remove the guinea fowl from the oven and spread over the breadcrumb mixture. Return to the oven and cook the guinea fowl, uncovered, for 20 minutes or until the breadcrumbs are golden and crisp.

To serve, remove the guinea fowl from the roasting tin. Add the beef jus to the tin and heat, stirring, to deglaze the tin. Strain the sauce and serve with the guinea fowl.

Duck with Pan-Fried Vegetables and a Red Onion Sauce

A simply stunning dish of vibrant colours and rich flavours.

INGREDIENTS FOR 4 SERVINGS

4 x 225 g (8 oz) DUCK BREASTS
1 tablespoon VEGETABLE OIL
100 g (4 oz) SMOKED STREAKY BACON, CHOPPED

FOR THE RED ONION SAUCE

2 tablespoons VEGETABLE OIL
2 LARGE RED ONIONS, SLICED
600 ml (1 pint) CHICKEN STOCK
375 ml (13 fl oz) RED WINE
SALT AND FRESHLY GROUND BLACK PEPPER

FOR THE PAN-FRIED VEGETABLES

8 BUTTON ONIONS, HALVED
8 BABY SWEETCORN, HALVED
175 g (6 oz) CARROTS, CUT INTO MATCHSTICKS

Pre-heat the oven to 180C/350F/Gas 4. To make the sauce, heat the oil in a saucepan, add the onions and cook for 7 minutes until lightly browned. Add the stock and wine and simmer until the sauce has reduced to 150 ml (¼ pint). Season and set aside.

To prepare the pan-fried vegetables, cook the button onions, baby sweetcorn and carrots in boiling salted water for about 5 minutes, until tender but still slightly crisp. Drain and set aside.

Score the skin of the duck breasts and season. Heat the oil in a frying pan until it begins to smoke then add the duck and cook until lightly browned on both sides. Transfer to a baking sheet and cook in the oven for 15 minutes.

Add the bacon to the frying pan and cook until golden and crisp. Add the drained vegetables and cook until browned. Remove from the pan with a slotted spoon and keep warm.

To serve, spoon the onion sauce on to warmed serving plates. Place the duck on top and arrange the vegetables and bacon around the duck.

Duck with Pan-Fried Vegetables and a Red Onion Sauce

ROASTING MEAT AND POULTRY

Successful roasting depends on the cut of the meat and the time and temperature for roasting. Modern methods for roasting meats include slow roasting at a low temperature, which reduces shrinkage and makes the joint more succulent. Quick roasting is done at higher temperatures and is more suitable for the better quality cuts of meat.

Here are instructions for both methods, and information on how to roast different cuts. If the joint or bird is stuffed, it is important to weigh it after stuffing when calculating the cooking time.

It is always best to let roast meat or poultry stand, or 'rest', for about 10 minutes after cooking – this makes it easier to carve.

CHICKEN AND TURKEY

The best quality chickens are free range.

To roast chicken, calculate the cooking time, allowing 20 minutes per 450 g (1 lb) plus 20 minutes. Preheat the oven to 200C/400F/Gas 6. Put the chicken on a rack above a roasting tin, to keep it out of the cooking juices, and roast, basting every 15 minutes to get a crispy skin. Allow to rest before carving.

To roast turkey, allow 20 minutes per 450 g (1 lb) plus 20 minutes. Pre-heat the oven to 180C/350F/Gas 4 and roast as for chicken. Because of the long cooking time needed for large birds, it may be necessary to cover the breast with foil to prevent over-browning. Allow to rest before carving.

ACCOMPANIMENTS

Serve roast chicken with a sage and onion stuffing, cooked separately to the bird, and a bread sauce.

Serve turkey with chestnut stuffing and cranberry sauce.

BEEF

The best cuts of beef for quick roasting are sirloin and rib, while topside and top rump are more suited for slow roasting.

To quick roast beef, allow 20 minutes per 450 g (1 lb), plus 20 minutes. Pre-heat the oven to 220C/425F/Gas 7. Roast the beef for 30 minutes then reduce the heat to 180C/350F/Gas 4 for the remaining roasting time.

To slow roast beef, allow 30 minutes per 450 g (1 lb), plus 30

minutes. Pre-heat the oven to 170C/325F/Gas 3 and roast the beef
for the calculated cooking time.

ACCOMPANIMENTS

Serve roast beef with Yorkshire pudding, horseradish sauce and
mustard gravy.

LAMB

The best cuts for roasting are the leg, loin and rack of lamb.

To quick roast lamb, allow 25 minutes per 450 g (1 lb), plus 25
minutes. Pre-heat the oven to 220C/425F/Gas 7. Roast the lamb for
30 minutes then reduce the heat to 180C/350F/Gas 4 for the
remaining roasting time.

To slow roast lamb, allow 40 minutes per 450 g (1 lb), plus 40
minutes. Pre-heat the oven to 170C/325F/Gas 3 and roast the lamb
for the calculated cooking time.

ACCOMPANIMENTS

Serve roast lamb with mint sauce or mint jelly, redcurrant jelly or
an apricot and walnut stuffing, formed into balls and cooked
separately.

VARIATIONS

Insert cloves of garlic and sprigs of rosemary into the lamb before
roasting. Coat the lamb with warmed honey to make a sticky glaze.
Coat the lamb with garlic oil and ground or fresh coriander.

PORK

The best cuts for roasting are fillet, leg and loin. Pork is not suitable
for slow roasting and must not be served rare. Roast pork is best
cooked on a rack.

To quick roast pork, allow 35 minutes per 450 g (1 lb), plus 35
minutes. Pre-heat the oven to 220C/425F/Gas 7. Roast for 30
minutes then reduce the heat to 180C/350F/Gas 4 for the remaining
roasting time.

ACCOMPANIMENTS

Serve roast pork with balls of sage and onion stuffing, apple sauce
or sage jelly.

To make crisp crackling, score the rind with a very sharp knife.
Brush with oil and rub with plenty of salt before roasting.

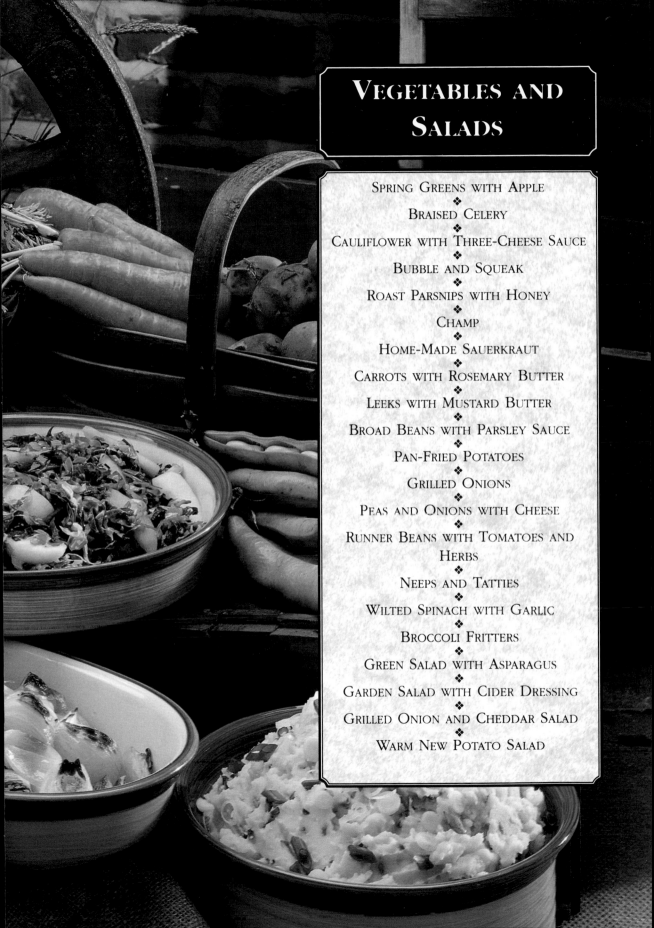

Vegetables and Salads

Spring Greens with Apple

❖

Braised Celery

❖

Cauliflower with Three-Cheese Sauce

❖

Bubble and Squeak

❖

Roast Parsnips with Honey

❖

Champ

❖

Home-Made Sauerkraut

❖

Carrots with Rosemary Butter

❖

Leeks with Mustard Butter

❖

Broad Beans with Parsley Sauce

❖

Pan-Fried Potatoes

❖

Grilled Onions

❖

Peas and Onions with Cheese

❖

Runner Beans with Tomatoes and Herbs

❖

Neeps and Tatties

❖

Wilted Spinach with Garlic

❖

Broccoli Fritters

❖

Green Salad with Asparagus

❖

Garden Salad with Cider Dressing

❖

Grilled Onion and Cheddar Salad

❖

Warm New Potato Salad

Spring Greens with Apple

A light, tasty accompaniment that goes particularly well with pork dishes.

Ingredients for 4 servings
450 g (1 lb) SPRING GREENS
175 g (6 oz) GRANNY SMITH'S APPLES
25 g (1 oz) BUTTER
SALT AND FRESHLY GROUND BLACK PEPPER

Remove any tough stalks from the spring greens, wash the leaves then thinly shred. Peel the apples, then core and slice.

Melt the butter in a large saucepan, gently stir in the apples and cook for 2 minutes until they start to colour. Increase the heat, add the spring greens and cook, stirring, for 2 minutes until just tender. Season and serve.

Variation
Add some spice by adding a 5 mm (¼ inch) piece of grated fresh root ginger to the pan with the apples.

Braised Celery

A simple dish that brings out the flavour of tender young celery hearts.

Ingredients for 4 servings
50 g (2 oz) BUTTER
1 GARLIC CLOVE, CRUSHED
1 SMALL ONION, FINELY CHOPPED
50 g (2 oz) CARROT, FINELY DICED
4 SMALL CELERY HEARTS
450 ml (¾ pint) CHICKEN STOCK
SALT AND FRESHLY GROUND BLACK PEPPER

Overleaf:
Roast Parsnips with Honey; Carrots with Rosemary Butter; Spring Greens with Apple; Grilled Onions; Champ.

108

Pre-heat the oven to 180C/350F/Gas 4. Melt the butter in a flameproof casserole. Add the garlic and cook for 1 minute.

Add the onion and carrot and cook gently, stirring occasionally, for 5 minutes until soft but not coloured.

Arrange the celery hearts on top and cover with the stock. Season. Cover and cook in the oven for about 1 hour, until the celery is tender.

To serve, remove the celery from the dish with a slotted spoon. Remove the diced vegetables with a slotted spoon and arrange on a serving dish. Place the celery on top.

CAULIFLOWER WITH THREE-CHEESE SAUCE

A rich, tasty version of cauliflower cheese.

INGREDIENTS FOR 4 SERVINGS

1 CAULIFLOWER
40 g (1½ oz) BUTTER
40 g (1½ oz) PLAIN FLOUR
450 ml (¾ pint) MILK
25 g (1 oz) CHESHIRE CHEESE, CRUMBLED
25 g (1 oz) CHEDDAR CHEESE, GRATED
SALT AND FRESHLY GROUND BLACK PEPPER
25 g (1 oz) LEICESTER CHEESE, GRATED

Break the cauliflower into small florets and cook in boiling salted water for 3–4 minutes. Drain.

Meanwhile, melt the butter in a large saucepan, add the flour and cook, stirring, for 1 minute. Gradually add the milk and heat gently, stirring, until thickened. Simmer for 2 minutes.

Pre-heat the grill. Add the Cheshire and Cheddar cheeses to the sauce and cook, stirring, until melted and well combined. Season. Add the cauliflower to the pan and stir to coat in the sauce. Transfer to a flameproof serving dish. Sprinkle with the Leicester cheese and grill until the cheese is melted and bubbling.

BUBBLE AND SQUEAK

Although you can use freshly cooked vegetables for this dish, it seems to taste even better when made with leftovers.

COOKING TIP
If you prefer, cook the potato mixture in one large cake. To turn, put a large plate over the pan and invert to turn the cake on to the plate. Add more butter and oil to the pan if necessary and slide the cake back into the pan. Cut into wedges to serve.

SERVING TIP
Serve the bubble and squeak as part of a traditional cooked breakfast.

INGREDIENTS FOR 4–6 SERVINGS

25 g (1 oz) BUTTER
175 g (6 oz) ONIONS, FINELY CHOPPED
450 g (1 lb) MASHED POTATOES
225 g (8 oz) COOKED GREEN CABBAGE
SALT AND FRESHLY GROUND BLACK PEPPER
50 ml (2 fl oz) VEGETABLE OIL

Heat half the butter in a frying pan, add the onions and cook for 5 minutes until soft but not coloured. In a bowl, combine the potatoes, cabbage, cooked onions and seasoning, mixing well.

Heat the remaining butter and the oil in a frying pan. Form the potato mixture into four cakes and add to the pan. Cook for about 5 minutes until the underside is golden. Turn and cook the other side for 5 minutes until golden. Serve immediately.

VARIATION
Sliced cooked Brussels sprouts can be used instead of the cabbage.

Bubble and Squeak

ROAST PARSNIPS WITH HONEY

Parsnips contain natural sugars which caramelize when they're roasted to give a rich, nutty flavour.

COOKING TIP
When measuring the honey, warm the spoon so the honey slips off easily. If the honey is thick, heat it gently in a small saucepan.

INGREDIENTS FOR 4 SERVINGS

2 tablespoons OLIVE OIL

50 g (2 oz) BUTTER

450 g (1 lb) PARSNIPS, CUT LENGTHWAYS INTO QUARTERS

2 tablespoons CLEAR HONEY

25 g (1 oz) FLAKED ALMONDS (OPTIONAL)

SALT AND FRESHLY GROUND BLACK PEPPER

Pre-heat the oven to 220C/425F/Gas 7. Put the oil and butter in a roasting tin and put in the oven to heat. As soon as a haze appears above the fat, add the parsnips, turn to coat in the fat and roast, turning occasionally for 20 minutes.

Pre-heat the grill. Brush the parsnips with the honey and sprinkle with the flaked almonds, if using. Grill until the honey starts to bubble.

To serve, transfer the parsnips to a serving dish and spoon the cooking juices over to give them an attractive glaze.

CHAMP

*This traditional Irish recipe can be served as a side dish or as a
light lunch.*

INGREDIENTS FOR 4 SERVINGS

450 g (1 lb) POTATOES, CUT INTO CHUNKS
50 g (2 oz) SHALLOTS, THINLY SLICED
½ BUNCH SPRING ONIONS, SLICED
150 ml (¼ pint) MILK
SALT AND FRESHLY GROUND BLACK PEPPER
2 tablespoons DOUBLE CREAM
25 g (1 oz) BUTTER

COOKING TIP
Save time and
energy by using a
food processor to
purée the
potatoes and
shallots.

SERVING TIP
Champ is often
served with a
pool of melted
butter in the
middle. Dip each
forkful of champ
into the butter as
you eat it.

Put the potatoes and shallots in a saucepan. Cover with cold water,
bring to the boil and cook for 15–20 minutes, until the potatoes are
tender. Drain, return to the saucepan and mash until smooth.

Meanwhile, reserve a few spring onion slices for garnish and
put the remainder in a saucepan with the milk. Bring to the boil
and cook for 2 minutes.

Add the milk and spring onion mixture to the mashed potato,
season and mix well. Stir in the cream and the butter. Return to the
heat and cook gently for 2 minutes to heat through.

Transfer to a warmed serving dish, sprinkle with the reserved
spring onion slices and serve.

VARIATIONS

Leek Champ: Omit the spring onions. Melt 15 g (½ oz) butter in a
frying pan and cook 150 g (5 oz) finely sliced leeks for 5 minutes,
until soft. Add to the milk and continue as above.

Cabbage Champ: Omit the spring onions. Finely shred 100 g
(4 oz) cabbage, add to the milk and continue as above.

HOME-MADE SAUERKRAUT

Sauerkraut is a type of pickled cabbage. This recipe from Gary Rhodes is the perfect accompaniment for his Boiled Collar of Bacon (see page 92) but goes just as well with pork chops or sausages.

INGREDIENTS FOR 4–6 SERVINGS

1 WHITE CABBAGE, FINELY SHREDDED
150 ml (¼ pint) WHITE WINE
150 ml (¼ pint) WHITE WINE VINEGAR
SALT AND FRESHLY GROUND BLACK PEPPER
25 g (1 oz) UNSALTED BUTTER
3 ONIONS, SLICED

FOR THE BOUQUET GARNI

2 teaspoons PICKLING SPICE
2 teaspoons JUNIPER BERRIES, LIGHTLY CRUSHED
PINCH OF DRIED THYME

To make the bouquet garni, tie the pickling spice, juniper berries and thyme in a piece of muslin.

Put the cabbage, wine and vinegar in a bowl with a good pinch of salt and the bouquet garni. Leave to marinate for 48 hours, turning occasionally to ensure the cabbage is well marinated.

Drain the cabbage, reserving the soaking liquor. Melt the butter in a saucepan, add the onions and cook until soft but not coloured.

Add the cabbage, bouquet garni and 2–3 tablespoons of the reserved soaking liquor. Cover and cook for 20 minutes, stirring occasionally and adding a little more liquor from time to time as it evaporates from the pan. When cooked, the cabbage should be tender but still have a slight bite. Season to taste. Serve with Boiled Collar of Bacon.

CARROTS WITH ROSEMARY BUTTER

Quick and simple to prepare, yet so much better than plain boiled carrots. If you can get baby carrots, all the better.

INGREDIENTS FOR 4 SERVINGS

50 g (2 oz) BUTTER
1 teaspoon FINELY CHOPPED FRESH ROSEMARY
SALT AND FRESHLY GROUND BLACK PEPPER
450 g (1 lb) CARROTS, THINLY SLICED
1 teaspoon SUGAR

Beat together the butter, rosemary and seasoning. Chill. Put the carrots, sugar and a knob of the rosemary butter in a saucepan of boiling salted water and cook for 10 minutes until just tender.

Drain the carrots, transfer to a warmed serving dish and top with shavings of rosemary butter.

LEEKS WITH MUSTARD BUTTER

This simple method of cooking leeks preserves all their flavour and goodness.

INGREDIENTS FOR 4 SERVINGS

25 g (1 oz) BUTTER, SOFTENED
½ teaspoon WHOLEGRAIN MUSTARD
1 dessertspoon VEGETABLE OIL
2 LEEKS, FINELY SHREDDED
SALT AND GROUND WHITE PEPPER

Beat together the butter and mustard and set aside.

Heat the oil in a frying pan over a high heat, add half the butter, then immediately add the leeks. Stir-fry for 2–3 minutes. Add the remaining butter, season and serve.

BROAD BEANS WITH
PARSLEY SAUCE

This classic combination just can't be bettered. It makes the perfect
accompaniment to gammon or ham.

INGREDIENTS FOR 4–6 SERVINGS

900 g (2 lb) BROAD BEANS IN THEIR PODS

FOR THE PARSLEY SAUCE

25 g (1 oz) BUTTER OR MARGARINE

50 g (2 oz) PLAIN FLOUR

300 ml (½ pint) CHICKEN STOCK

150 ml (¼ pint) SINGLE CREAM

2 tablespoons FINELY CHOPPED FRESH PARSLEY

2 EGG YOLKS

SALT AND FRESHLY GROUND BLACK PEPPER

Shell the beans and cook in a saucepan of boiling water for about 15 minutes, until tender. If liked, remove some of the beans from the pan after about 2 minutes. Leave to cool slightly, then peel away the outer skin (see page 57).

Meanwhile, make the sauce. Melt the butter in a saucepan, add the flour and cook, stirring, for 1 minute. Gradually add the stock, stirring to form a smooth sauce. Add the cream and cook gently for 5 minutes, stirring occasionally.

Remove the sauce from the heat, add the parsley and beat in the egg yolks. Season.

Drain the beans and transfer to a serving dish. Add the peeled beans, if using. Pour the sauce over the beans and serve.

VARIATION

To turn this dish into a delicious light meal, add 50 g (2 oz) grated mature Cheddar cheese to the sauce just before removing it from the heat. Heat gently, stirring, until the cheese has melted into the sauce. Continue as above.

Broad Beans with Parsley Sauce

PAN-FRIED POTATOES

Try this recipe for a simple yet delicious alternative to chips.

INGREDIENTS FOR 4 SERVINGS

900 g (2 lb) EVEN-SIZED POTATOES, WASHED
25 g (1 oz) UNSALTED BUTTER
2 tablespoons VEGETABLE OIL
SALT AND FRESHLY GROUND BLACK PEPPER

Put the unpeeled potatoes in a saucepan of cold salted water, bring to the boil and cook for 10–15 minutes, until the potatoes are cooked but still firm. Peel the potatoes while they are still hot and cut into 5 mm (¼ inch) slices.

Heat the butter and oil in a large frying pan until very hot. Put the potatoes in a single layer in the pan and cook until the underside is golden. Turn them over and cook the other side until golden. Remove from the pan, season well and serve immediately.

VARIATIONS

Pan-Fried Potatoes with Garlic and Mustard: Infuse the vegetable oil with a cracked garlic clove for a few hours. Remove the garlic. Boil and peel the potatoes as above. Heat the butter and garlic oil and add 1 teaspoon of English mustard. Add the potatoes and continue as above.

Pan-Fried Potatoes with Vegetables: Thinly slice 100 g (4 oz) red onions, leeks or mushrooms and lightly fry in a separate pan. Sprinkle over the cooked potatoes just before serving.

Pan-Fried Potatoes with Tomato Sauce: In a separate pan, cook 25 g (1 oz) finely diced onion, 1 crushed garlic clove, 2 chopped tomatoes and 1 tablespoon tomato purée. Serve with the potatoes.

GRILLED ONIONS

A ridged grill pan is a great way to char-grill vegetables without the fuss of a barbecue.

INGREDIENTS FOR 4 SERVINGS

2 ONIONS
1 tablespoon OLIVE OIL
SALT AND FRESHLY GROUND BLACK PEPPER

Cut each onion into eight even-sized wedges. Heat a ridged grill pan until moderately hot and arrange the onion wedges on it. Brush them lightly with the oil and grill for about 5 minutes on each side or until they are just tender. Season and serve.

PEAS AND ONIONS WITH CHEESE

A topping of grated Cheddar adds the finishing touch to a tasty combination of fresh peas and tiny onions.

INGREDIENTS FOR 4 SERVINGS

350 g (12 oz) FRESH SHELLED PEAS
100 g (4 oz) PICKLING ONIONS
15 g (½ oz) BUTTER
½ teaspoon CHOPPED FRESH CHERVIL
1 tablespoon FINELY GRATED CHEDDAR CHEESE
SALT AND FRESHLY GROUND BLACK PEPPER

Put the peas and onions in a saucepan of boiling water, reduce the heat and simmer for 10–15 minutes until tender. Drain.

Melt the butter in a separate saucepan, add the peas and onions and stir to coat in the butter. Stir in the chervil and cheese and season to taste. Serve immediately.

BUYING TIP
You will need about 700 g (1½ lb) peas in their pods to give 350 g (12 oz) shelled peas.

COOKING TIP
Frozen peas can be used instead of fresh. Cook the onions for about 8 minutes until just tender, then add the peas and simmer for 2 minutes. Continue as in the recipe.

RUNNER BEANS WITH TOMATOES AND HERBS

Use the best quality fresh ingredients for this summer-time dish.

INGREDIENTS FOR 4 SERVINGS

450 g (1 lb) RUNNER BEANS, SLICED
1 tablespoon VEGETABLE OIL
1 GARLIC CLOVE, CRUSHED
1 ONION, FINELY CHOPPED
225 g (8 oz) RIPE TOMATOES, PEELED AND CHOPPED
SALT AND FRESHLY GROUND BLACK PEPPER
CHOPPED FRESH BASIL AND PARSLEY, TO GARNISH

Put the runner beans into a saucepan of boiling salted water and cook for 5–7 minutes until tender. Drain.

Heat the oil in a saucepan, add the garlic and onion and cook, stirring occasionally, for 3 minutes until soft but not coloured. Stir in the tomatoes, then the beans and heat gently to warm through. Season well, sprinkle with the herbs and serve.

VARIATION

Runner Beans with Croûtons: Infuse 75 ml (3 fl oz) vegetable oil with a cracked garlic clove for a few hours. Remove the garlic. Cook the runner beans in boiling salted water as above. Remove the crusts from 3 slices of white bread and cut the bread into cubes. Heat the garlic oil in a frying pan, add the bread cubes and fry, turning, until golden brown all over. Mix the croûtons with the cooked beans and serve.

Runner Beans with Tomatoes and Herbs

NEEPS AND TATTIES

In Scotland, swedes are called neeps. This dish is a traditional accompaniment to haggis.

INGREDIENTS FOR 4 SERVINGS

450 g (1 lb) POTATOES, DICED

450 g (1 lb) SWEDE, DICED

75 g (3 oz) BUTTER

75 ml (3 fl oz) SINGLE CREAM

SALT AND FRESHLY GROUND BLACK PEPPER

50 ml (2 fl oz) DOUBLE CREAM

Put the potatoes in a saucepan of cold salted water, bring to the boil and cook for 15 minutes until tender. Put the swede in a saucepan of cold salted water, bring to the boil and cook for 15–20 minutes until tender. Drain, keeping each vegetable separate.

Mash or purée the potatoes with half the butter and single cream. In a separate bowl, mash or purée the swede with the remaining butter and single cream. Combine the potato and swede and season with salt and plenty of freshly ground black pepper.

To serve, transfer the mixture to a warmed serving dish. Warm the double cream and pour over the neeps and tatties.

VARIATIONS

Flavour the mashed vegetables with chopped fresh thyme or crushed garlic.

WILTED SPINACH WITH GARLIC

Young spinach leaves lightly cooked in garlic-flavoured oil.

INGREDIENTS FOR 4 SERVINGS

1	GARLIC CLOVE
2 teaspoons	VEGETABLE OIL
350 g (12 oz)	YOUNG SPINACH, TRIMMED AND WASHED

Peel the garlic clove, then crack it with the back of a knife, to release the juices. Put the oil in a small bowl, add the garlic and leave to infuse for a few hours.

Strain the oil, discarding the garlic. Heat the garlic oil in a frying pan or small wok over a high heat. Add the spinach and stir fry for 2–3 minutes until the spinach wilts. Serve.

> **INGREDIENTS TIP**
> You can replace some or all of the spinach with finely chopped watercress and spring greens.

BROCCOLI FRITTERS

Crisp broccoli florets coated in the lightest of batters.

INGREDIENTS FOR 4 SERVINGS

	VEGETABLE OIL FOR DEEP FRYING
3	EGG WHITES
3 tablespoons	PLAIN FLOUR
	SALT AND GROUND WHITE PEPPER
350 g (12 oz)	BROCCOLI, CUT INTO FLORETS

Put the vegetable oil in a deep-fat fryer or large saucepan and heat to 185C/360F.

Whisk the egg whites until stiff. Sift the flour into a polythene bag and season with salt and pepper. Put the broccoli florets into the flour, a few at a time, and shake the bag to coat with flour. Dip the florets into the egg white.

Immediately lower the broccoli into the oil, in batches if necessary, and fry for 2–3 minutes. Drain on kitchen paper and keep warm while frying the remainder. Sprinkle with salt and serve.

> **SERVING TIP**
> Serve the fritters as quickly as possible, otherwise they will go soft.

Green Salad with Asparagus

A simple salad made with high-quality ingredients.

Ingredients for 4 servings

8 ASPARAGUS SPEARS
SALAD LEAVES, INCLUDING FRISEE, COS, LAMB'S
LETTUCE AND BABY SPINACH LEAVES

For the dressing

1 HARD-BOILED EGG
4 dessertspoons WALNUT OIL
4 WALNUTS, CHOPPED
SALT

Bring a saucepan of salted water to a rapid boil, add the asparagus spears and cook for 2 minutes, then immediately plunge into iced water to stop further cooking.

Put the salad leaves in a serving bowl. Drain the asparagus spears and cut into 2.5 cm (1 inch) lengths. Add to the bowl.

To make the dressing, cut the egg in half and remove the yolk. Chop the egg white and put in a small bowl with the oil, walnuts and salt. Put the egg yolk into a sieve and push through the sieve into the dressing. Mix together. Pour over the salad and serve.

Variation

Omit the hard-boiled egg from the dressing. Cut 4 hard-boiled quail's eggs lengthways in half and add to the salad with the asparagus. Continue as above.

Green Salad with Asparagus

GARDEN SALAD WITH CIDER DRESSING

A simple, fresh-tasting salad of traditional ingredients served with a tasty cider dressing.

SERVING TIP
Salad ingredients can be prepared in advance and stored in the refrigerator but, to keep their freshness, don't pour over the dressing until you are ready to serve.

INGREDIENTS FOR 4 SERVINGS

2 LITTLE GEM LETTUCES

8 cm (3 inch) PIECE OF CUCUMBER, PEELED AND DICED

3 CELERY STICKS, SLICED

1 BUNCH OF WATERCRESS

4 TOMATOES, QUARTERED

6 RADISHES, SLICED

FOR THE DRESSING

1 tablespoon SUNFLOWER OIL

2 tablespoons DRY CIDER

1 teaspoon FINELY CHOPPED FRESH THYME

1 teaspoon FINELY CHOPPED FRESH ROSEMARY

1 teaspoon SNIPPED FRESH CHIVES

SALT AND FRESHLY GROUND BLACK PEPPER

Arrange all the salad ingredients in a serving bowl.

Whisk together all the ingredients for the dressing and spoon over the salad. Toss gently and serve immediately.

Garden Salad with Cider Dressing

GRILLED ONION AND CHEDDAR SALAD

Cheddar cheese and onion combine so well, why not try them in this delightful salad.

INGREDIENTS FOR 4 SERVINGS

2	LARGE ONIONS, SLICED
2	RED ONIONS, SLICED
1 tablespoon	OLIVE OIL
	SALAD LEAVES, INCLUDING WATERCRESS, LAMB'S LETTUCE AND FRISEE
75 g (3 oz)	MATURE FARMHOUSE CHEDDAR CHEESE
	THYME, PARSLEY AND BASIL SPRIGS, TO GARNISH

FOR THE DRESSING

2 tablespoons	OLIVE OIL
1 tablespoon	BALSAMIC VINEGAR

Pre-heat the grill. Put the onion slices on a grill rack, drizzle with the oil and grill under a moderate to high heat for about 5 minutes, turning once. Leave to cool.

Arrange the salad leaves in a serving bowl.

Separate the onion rings and arrange on top of the salad leaves. Using a vegetable peeler, shave the cheese on to the salad. Sprinkle with the oil and balsamic vinegar, garnish with small sprigs of herbs and serve immediately.

WARM NEW POTATO SALAD

A delicious summer salad of warm new potatoes tossed in a nutty dressing.

INGREDIENTS FOR 4 SERVINGS

450 g (1 lb) NEW POTATOES, SCRUBBED
50 ml (2 fl oz) OLIVE OIL, WARMED
SALT AND FRESHLY GROUND BLACK PEPPER

FOR THE DRESSING

1 tablespoon WHITE WINE VINEGAR
3 tablespoons SUNFLOWER OIL
2 tablespoons HAZELNUT OIL

Cook the potatoes in a saucepan of boiling salted water for 15 minutes until just tender. Drain, slice and place in a serving bowl while still warm. Drizzle with the olive oil and season. Cover and keep warm.

Combine all the ingredients for the dressing and heat gently until just warm. Add to the potatoes and gently toss the potatoes in the dressing, to coat. Serve immediately.

PUDDINGS AND DESSERTS

SUMMER PUDDINGS

All the flavours of a British summer contained in a bread case that's soaked with the ruby-red fruit juices.

INGREDIENTS FOR 4 INDIVIDUAL PUDDINGS

100 g (4 oz) REDCURRANTS
100 g (4 oz) BLACKCURRANTS
100 g (4 oz) STRAWBERRIES
100 g (4 oz) RASPBERRIES
25 g (1 oz) SUGAR
8 THIN SLICES WHITE BREAD, CRUSTS REMOVED
4 MINT LEAVES
ICING SUGAR FOR DUSTING

Reserve some of the fruit for decoration. Remove the currants from the stalks. Cut the strawberries into wedges. Put all the fruit and the sugar into a saucepan with just enough water to cover. Bring to the boil and simmer gently for 5–6 minutes, adjusting the sweetness if required. Drain, reserving the cooking liquid.

Cut four rounds from the bread to fit the bases of four 150 ml (¼ pint) dariole moulds. Cut out four rounds to fit the tops of the moulds. Cut the remaining bread into fingers to fit up the sides of the moulds.

Take the rounds of bread for the bases, dip them in the reserved cooking liquid and place in the moulds. Dip the fingers of bread in the liquid and use to line the sides of the moulds, ensuring there are no gaps. Divide the fruit among the moulds so that it fills them.

Dip the remaining rounds of bread into the liquid and put on top of the puddings, pressing them down. Cover the dishes with baking parchment, put a weight on each dish and chill for at least 2 hours, preferably overnight. Strain the remaining liquid and chill.

To serve, carefully turn out the puddings on to serving plates and spoon over a little of the strained liquor. Arrange the reserved fruit around the puddings and decorate with mint leaves and a dusting of icing sugar.

Overleaf:
Summer Pudding;
Bread and Butter
Pudding;
Strawberries and
Cream with
Chocolate
Shortbread.

STRAWBERRIES AND CREAM WITH CHOCOLATE SHORTBREAD

An impressive dessert full of everyone's favourite ingredients.

INGREDIENTS FOR 4 SERVINGS
FOR THE CHOCOLATE SHORTBREAD

50 g (2 oz)	PLAIN FLOUR
25 g (1 oz)	FINE SEMOLINA
25 g (1 oz)	CASTER SUGAR
50 g (2 oz)	BUTTER, SOFTENED
1 teaspoon	COCOA POWDER
	ICING SUGAR FOR DUSTING
	CHOCOLATE CURLS, TO DECORATE

FOR THE FILLING

350 g (12 oz)	STRAWBERRIES, HULLED AND SLICED
300 ml (½ pint)	DOUBLE CREAM, WHIPPED

COOKING TIPS

If you prefer, you can make thicker shortbreads and sandwich them together in twos. They will need a longer cooking time – about 10–12 minutes.

To make chocolate curls, use a vegetable peeler to shave curls off the edge of a block of chocolate. For best results, the chocolate should be chilled.

Pre-heat the oven to 170C/325F/Gas 3. Line a baking sheet with baking parchment.

To make the chocolate shortbread, put all the ingredients in a bowl and beat together to form a smooth paste. Put the dough between two sheets of baking parchment and thinly roll out.

Remove the top piece of baking parchment and cut out twelve rounds of shortbread with a pastry cutter. Use a palette knife to transfer the rounds to the baking sheet and bake for 5 minutes. Transfer to a wire rack and leave to cool.

Spoon a little whipped cream on to four shortbread rounds. Top with some strawberry slices. Add another layer of shortbread, cream and strawberries. Top with a third shortbread round. Dust with sifted icing sugar, decorate with chocolate curls and serve.

BREAD AND BUTTER PUDDING

*Slices of French bread set in a wickedly rich custard makes a
delightful conclusion to any meal.*

INGREDIENTS FOR 4–6 SERVINGS

50 g (2 oz)	BUTTER, SOFTENED
24	THIN SLICES FRENCH BREAD
8	EGG YOLKS
150 g (5 oz)	CASTER SUGAR
1	VANILLA POD
300 ml (½ pint)	FULL-FAT MILK
300 ml (½ pint)	DOUBLE CREAM
50 g (2 oz)	SULTANAS
1 tablespoon	APRICOT JAM OR ICING SUGAR, TO FINISH

Pre-heat the oven to 170C/325F/Gas 3. Spread the butter on to one
side of each slice of bread. Whisk together the egg yolks and sugar
in a bowl. Put the vanilla pod, milk and cream in a saucepan and
bring to the boil. Remove the vanilla pod and whisk the milk and
cream into the egg and sugar mixture.

Arrange the bread, butter side up, in neat layers in an ovenproof
dish, sprinkling each layer with the sultanas. Carefully pour the
custard over the bread and leave to stand for 30 minutes. Put the
dish in a roasting tin and pour enough warm water into the tin to
come three-quarters of the way up the side of the pudding dish.

Bake for about 30 minutes, until the custard has set. Remove
from the oven and take the dish out of the roasting tin.

Warm the apricot jam then brush it over the top of the pudding.
Alternatively, sprinkle the pudding with icing sugar, then put under
a pre-heated hot grill until the icing sugar bubbles and just begins
to caramelize, being careful not to burn the crust. Serve
immediately with ice cream or cream.

PANCAKES WITH STEWED GOOSEBERRIES

A truly British filling for rich golden pancakes.

INGREDIENTS FOR 6–8 SERVINGS

FOR THE PANCAKES

100 g (4 oz)	PLAIN FLOUR
	PINCH OF SALT
2	EGGS, BEATEN
1 tablespoon	BRANDY
300 ml (½ pint)	SINGLE CREAM
25 g (1 oz)	BUTTER, MELTED
	VEGETABLE OIL FOR FRYING
	VANILLA OR CINNAMON SUGAR FOR DUSTING

FOR THE FILLING

300 ml (½ pint)	WATER
50 ml (2 fl oz)	ELDERFLOWER CORDIAL
225 g (8 oz)	SUGAR
900 g (2 lb)	GOOSEBERRIES, TOPPED AND TAILED

> **COOKING TIPS**
> A small non-stick pan is best for cooking pancakes.
>
> Make sure you use a mildly flavoured oil so it doesn't flavour the pancakes. You only need a small amount of oil – wipe around the pan with kitchen paper to remove any excess before adding the batter

To make the pancakes, put the flour, salt, eggs, brandy and cream into a bowl and whisk together to form a smooth batter. Whisk in the melted butter. Leave to stand while you prepare the filling.

Put the water, cordial and sugar into a saucepan and bring to the boil. Add the gooseberries and simmer for about 15 minutes until they are tender but still keep their shape.

Heat a crêpe pan or small frying pan and coat very lightly with oil. Pour in enough batter to cover the pan in a thin layer, tilting the pan to give an even layer of batter. Cook for 10–15 seconds until the underside is golden. Turn and cook for a further 10–15 seconds. Transfer to a warmed plate and keep warm while making the remainder, stacking them as they are cooked. Continue until you have two pancakes per serving.

To serve, lay a pancake on a serving plate, place a little fruit in the centre and fold over. Repeat with a second pancake. Dust with vanilla sugar and serve with cream or ice cream.

BURNT CAMBRIDGE CREAMS

A delicious version of this classic dessert; stewed rhubarb under a set cream with a crisp caramel topping.

ANTONY WORRALL THOMPSON

This recipe by Antony Worrall Thompson was featured in the Gardner Merchant Master Class '95.

COOKING TIP
The creams must be very cold before you grill the sugar, otherwise the cream will separate. Make sure the grill is as hot as possible.

INGREDIENTS FOR 4 SERVINGS
FOR THE RHUBARB BASE

275 g (10 oz)	RHUBARB, CUT INTO 2.5 CM (1 INCH) PIECES
25 ml (1 fl oz)	FRESH ORANGE JUICE
	CASTER SUGAR, TO TASTE
	GRATED ZEST OF $\frac{1}{2}$ ORANGE
	GRATED ZEST OF $\frac{1}{2}$ LEMON
1 dessertspoon	DICED STEM GINGER

FOR THE CREAM

4	LARGE EGG YOLKS
600 ml (1 pint)	DOUBLE CREAM
	CASTER SUGAR, FOR SPRINKLING

To make the rhubarb base, put all the ingredients in a heavy-based saucepan and cook over a gentle heat for a few minutes until the rhubarb is soft but not mushy. Set aside.

To make the cream, whisk the egg yolks in a bowl. Put the cream in a saucepan and bring to the boil. Boil for about 30 seconds then immediately pour on to the egg yolks and whisk together. Return the mixture to the pan and heat gently, stirring, without allowing it to boil, until it thickens and coats the back of the spoon.

Put a little of the rhubarb into each of four small ramekins and pour on the cream mixture. Chill the creams overnight.

Two hours before serving, pre-heat the grill to maximum. Sprinkle the creams with an even layer of caster sugar and grill until the sugar melts and caramelizes to a light brown colour. Leave to cool then chill until required.

VARIATIONS

Use other fruits, such as apple, gooseberry or a mixture of fruits.

For a special occasion, serve this dessert as it was served at the Master Class: each guest had three mini burnt creams, each with a different fruit in the base.

Burnt Cambridge Creams

APPLE AND CHEDDAR CHEESE PIE

The ever-popular combination of apples and cheese is given a new twist in this sweet pie.

> **COOKING TIP**
> The layer of semolina at the bottom of the pie helps keep the pastry crisp during cooking.

INGREDIENTS FOR 6–8 SERVINGS

FOR THE PASTRY

175 g (6 oz) SELF-RAISING FLOUR
50 g (2 oz) WHOLEMEAL FLOUR
100 g (4 oz) BUTTER, DICED
50 g (2 oz) MATURE CHEDDAR CHEESE, GRATED
2 EGG YOLKS
2 dessertspoons COLD WATER
BEATEN EGG FOR GLAZING

FOR THE FILLING

700 g (1½ lb) BRAMLEY APPLES
15 g (½ oz) SEMOLINA
75 g (3 oz) SOFT BROWN SUGAR
PINCH OF GROUND CINNAMON

TO FINISH

25g (1 oz) MATURE CHEDDAR CHEESE, GRATED

To make the pastry, sift the two flours into a large bowl. Add the butter and cheese and rub into the flour. Add the egg yolks and water and gently mix together to form a smooth dough. Wrap the dough in cling film and chill for at least 30 minutes.

Meanwhile, peel, quarter and core the apples then slice very finely. Pre-heat the oven to 180C/350F/Gas 4.

Roll out three-quarters of the pastry on a lightly floured surface and use to line a 23 cm (9 inch) loose-bottomed flan tin. Sprinkle the semolina over the pastry. Arrange the apple slices on top of the pastry and sprinkle with the sugar and cinnamon.

Roll out the remaining pastry and use to cover the pie. Seal the edges well. Glaze the pastry with beaten egg. Make a small hole in the centre of the pie with a small knife, to allow steam to escape. Bake for 40–45 minutes.

To finish, sprinkle the pie with grated cheese and serve hot.

GYPSY TART

This pudding is so easy to make and uses ingredients you are likely to have in your store cupboard. It is often eaten with wedges of apple.

INGREDIENTS FOR 8–10 SERVINGS

FOR THE PASTRY

225 g (8 oz) PLAIN FLOUR
100 g (4 oz) BUTTER OR MARGARINE
2–3 tablespoons COLD WATER

FOR THE FILLING

410 g (14 oz) can EVAPORATED MILK
350 g (12 oz) DARK SOFT BROWN SUGAR
1 tablespoon STRAWBERRY JAM, WARMED

To make the pastry, sift the flour into a bowl and rub in the butter or margarine until the mixture resembles fine breadcrumbs. Add sufficient cold water to bind to a smooth dough. Wrap in cling film and chill for 30 minutes.

Pre-heat the oven to 200C/400F/Gas 6. Roll out the pastry on a lightly floured surface and use to line a 25 cm (10 inch) flan tin. Line the pastry case with baking parchment, fill with dried peas or beans and bake blind for 15 minutes. Remove the paper and beans and leave to cool slightly. Spread the jam over the pastry case.

Meanwhile, make the filling. Use an electric whisk to whisk together the evaporated milk and sugar until the mixture has doubled in quantity and is creamy in texture. (This can take up to 10 minutes.) Pour the mixture into the pastry case and bake for 10–15 minutes until the mixture is just set and lightly browned.

Leave to cool before serving.

RIPE TART

A traditional favourite from the South-East of England.

<table>
<tr><td>

INGREDIENTS TIP
In the winter months, replace the fresh cherries with morello cherries, often sold in large jars. Make sure you don't buy cherries in a thick syrup. Drain and dry on kitchen paper before use.

</td></tr>
</table>

INGREDIENTS FOR 4–6 SERVINGS

FOR THE PASTRY

175 g (6 oz) PLAIN FLOUR

75 g (3 oz) BUTTER OR MARGARINE

1 tablespoon CASTER SUGAR

PINCH OF SALT

1 EGG, BEATEN

FOR THE FILLING

450 g (1 lb) FRESH CHERRIES, STONED

100 g (4 oz) ICING SUGAR

75 g (3 oz) GROUND ALMONDS

2 EGGS

FEW DROPS OF ALMOND ESSENCE

To make the pastry, sift the flour into a bowl and rub in the butter or margarine until the mixture resembles fine breadcrumbs. Stir in the sugar and salt. Add the egg and mix to form a smooth dough. Wrap in cling film and chill for 30 minutes.

Pre-heat the oven to 170C/325F/Gas 3. Roll out the pastry on a lightly floured surface and use to line a 20 cm (8 inch) flan tin.

To make the filling, arrange the cherries in the pastry case. Beat together the icing sugar, ground almonds, eggs and almond essence. Pour into the pastry case, to cover the cherries.

Bake for about 45 minutes, until the almond mixture is golden and set. Serve warm or cold, with soured cream.

Ripe Tart

BAKEWELL TART

A crisp pastry case filled with raspberry jam and a light almond sponge – a perennial favourite.

INGREDIENTS FOR 6–8 SERVINGS

FOR THE PASTRY

175 g (6 oz)	PLAIN FLOUR
75 g (3 oz)	BUTTER OR MARGARINE
1 tablespoon	CASTER SUGAR
	PINCH OF SALT
1	EGG, BEATEN

FOR THE FILLING

4 tablespoons	RASPBERRY OR STRAWBERRY JAM
50 g (2 oz)	BUTTER, SOFTENED
100 g (4 oz)	CASTER SUGAR
100 g (4 oz)	GROUND ALMONDS
3	EGGS, BEATEN
¼ teaspoon	ALMOND ESSENCE
	ICING SUGAR FOR DUSTING
	TOASTED FLAKED ALMONDS, TO DECORATE

To make the pastry, sift the flour into a bowl and rub in the butter or margarine until the mixture resembles fine breadcrumbs. Stir in the sugar and salt. Add the egg and mix to form a smooth dough. Wrap in cling film and chill for 30 minutes.

Pre-heat the oven to 200C/400F/Gas 6. Roll out the pastry on a lightly floured surface and use to line a 20 cm (8 inch) flan tin. Spread the jam over the pastry base. Chill while making the filling.

To make the filling, beat together the butter, sugar, almonds, eggs and almond essence for 5 minutes. Spoon the filling into the pastry case and level the top. Bake for 30 minutes, until the filling is set. Leave to cool slightly. Dust with icing sugar, decorate with toasted almonds and serve hot or cold with cream or custard.

TREACLE TART

This sticky delight will instantly remind you of your childhood favourites.

INGREDIENTS FOR 6–8 SERVINGS

FOR THE PASTRY

225 g (8 oz) PLAIN FLOUR

100 g (4 oz) BUTTER OR MARGARINE

1 tablespoon CASTER SUGAR

PINCH OF SALT

1 EGG, BEATEN

BEATEN EGG FOR GLAZING

FOR THE FILLING

225 g (8 oz) GOLDEN SYRUP

FINELY GRATED ZEST OF 1 LEMON

1 teaspoon FRESH LEMON JUICE

75 g (3 oz) FRESH WHITE BREADCRUMBS

> **COOKING TIP**
> The easiest way to measure golden syrup is to put the saucepan on your scales, set them at zero, then measure the syrup directly into the saucepan. Use a warmed spoon so the syrup slides off easily.

To make the pastry, sift the flour into a bowl and rub in the butter or margarine until the mixture resembles fine breadcrumbs. Stir in the sugar and salt. Add the egg and a little cold water and mix to form a smooth dough. Wrap in cling film and chill for 30 minutes.

Pre-heat the oven to 190C/375F/Gas 5. Roll out the pastry on a lightly floured surface and use to line a 20 cm (8 inch) flan tin. Reserve the pastry trimmings.

To make the filling, put the syrup, lemon zest and juice in a saucepan and heat gently until the syrup has melted. Stir in the breadcrumbs. Carefully spread into the pastry case.

Roll out the pastry trimmings and cut into 5 mm (¼ inch) wide strips. Arrange on top of the tart in a lattice pattern. Brush with the beaten egg. Bake for about 25 minutes until the filling is just set and the pastry is golden. Serve warm or cold.

VARIATION

If you prefer, replace half the golden syrup with dark treacle, for an authentic treacle tart.

SWEET YORKSHIRE PUDDINGS WITH PLUM COMPOTE

Forget the traditional way of serving Yorkshire puddings and give them a new lease of life in this delicious dessert.

INGREDIENTS FOR 6–8 SERVINGS
FOR THE YORKSHIRE PUDDINGS

75 ml (3 fl oz)	PLAIN FLOUR
2	EGGS, BEATEN
1 tablespoon	GROUND ALMONDS
1 tablespoon	CASTER SUGAR
75 ml (3 fl oz)	MILK
	GRATED ZEST OF $\frac{1}{2}$ ORANGE
	VEGETABLE OIL FOR BRUSHING
	ICING SUGAR, FLAKED ALMONDS AND STRIPS OF PARED ORANGE ZEST, TO DECORATE
	VANILLA ICE CREAM, TO SERVE

FOR THE PLUM COMPOTE

350 g (12 oz)	PLUMS, STONED AND SLICED
75 g (3 oz)	SUGAR
	PINCH OF GROUND CINNAMON

To make the Yorkshire puddings, sift the flour into a bowl. Add the eggs, ground almonds, sugar, milk and orange zest and mix to form a smooth batter. Leave to stand for 30 minutes.

Pre-heat the oven to 220C/425F/Gas 7. Brush small Yorkshire pudding tins with a little vegetable oil and put in the oven to heat. Divide the batter among the tins and bake for 15–20 minutes until risen and golden.

Meanwhile, make the plum compôte. Put all the ingredients in a saucepan and cook gently for 5 minutes, until the plums are tender but retain their shape.

To serve, put a Yorkshire pudding on each serving plate. Add a scoop of ice cream and the plum compôte. Sprinkle with almonds, dust with icing sugar and decorate with orange zest.

Sweet Yorkshire Puddings with Plum Compôte

SPOTTED DICK

Old-fashioned puddings are experiencing a revival, and this steamed suet roll has to be one of the best.

<table>
<tr><td>

COOKING TIP
For extra flavour, soak the currants overnight in sweet sherry. Drain before adding to the dry ingredients.

</td></tr>
</table>

INGREDIENTS FOR 4–6 SERVINGS

75 g (3 oz) SELF-RAISING FLOUR

100 g (4 oz) FRESH WHITE BREADCRUMBS

50 g (2 oz) CASTER SUGAR

75 g (3 oz) SHREDDED SUET

FINELY GRATED ZEST OF 1 LEMON

175 g (6 oz) CURRANTS

150 ml (¼ pint) MILK

Sift the flour into a bowl and stir in the other dry ingredients. Add sufficient milk to make a smooth, elastic dough. Turn the dough on to a lightly floured surface and shape into a neat roll about 15 cm (6 inches) long.

Put a large piece of baking parchment on top of a large piece of foil and make a pleat across the centre to allow the pudding to expand. Put the pudding on top and wrap the parchment and foil around the pudding, folding the edges together to seal.

Put in a large saucepan of boiling water, making sure the pudding is well covered with water. Alternatively, put in a steamer. Cover and cook for 1½ hours. Unwrap the pudding, slice and serve with custard.

TOFFEE APPLE PUDDING

A toffee-coated suet crust conceals a filling of stewed apples in this sticky treat.

INGREDIENTS FOR 4–6 SERVINGS
FOR THE SUET PASTRY

225 g (8 oz) SELF-RAISING FLOUR

PINCH OF SALT

100 g (4 oz) VEGETABLE SUET

150–300 ml (¼–½ pint) MILK

FOR THE FILLING

75–100 g (3–4 oz) SOFT BROWN SUGAR

75–175 g (3–6 oz) BUTTER

700 g (1½ lb) COOKING APPLES, PEELED, CORED AND SLICED

2 tablespoons APPLE JUICE OR WATER

> **COOKING TIP**
> The layer of butter and sugar on the basin makes the toffee part of the pudding – the more toffee you like the thicker you should make the layer.

To make the pastry, sift the flour and salt into a bowl and stir in the suet. Gradually add enough milk to form a light, elastic dough, stirring it in with a palette knife. Turn on to a lightly floured surface and knead lightly until smooth.

Spread a thick layer of butter on the base and sides of a 1.1 litre (2 pint) pudding basin. Sprinkle with a thick layer of brown sugar. Roll out three-quarters of the pastry and use to line the basin. Put the apples into the lined basin and add the apple juice or water. Add brown sugar to taste. Roll out the remaining pastry to make a lid and cover the pudding, sealing the edges well

Cover the pudding with a piece of pleated greased baking parchment then a piece of pleated foil. Secure with string. Put the basin in a large saucepan and add enough boiling water to come halfway up the basin. Alternatively, put in a steamer. Cover and steam for 2 hours, topping up with more boiling water if necessary.

Carefully turn the pudding on to a warmed serving plate and serve with custard.

ORANGE, BRANDY AND MARMALADE STEAMED PUDDING

A delicious citrus-flavoured steamed pudding, smothered in an orange and brandy sauce.

<table>
<tr><td colspan="2" align="center">PREPARATION TIP</td></tr>
</table>

> **PREPARATION TIP**
> Be careful to avoid the bitter pith when you pare the rind from the orange. You can buy special utensils which pare strips of rind directly from the fruit.

INGREDIENTS FOR 4–6 SERVINGS

1	ORANGE
2 tablespoons	BRANDY
4 heaped tablespoons	MARMALADE
75 g (3 oz)	BUTTER
75 g (3 oz)	CASTER SUGAR
1	EGG, BEATEN
175 g (6 oz)	SELF-RAISING FLOUR
	PINCH OF SALT
75 ml (3 fl oz)	MILK

Pare the zest from the orange, then cut the zest into fine strips. Blanch the strips of orange zest in a saucepan of boiling water for 2 minutes. Drain, rinse in cold water and dry on kitchen paper.

Peel the pith from the orange. Working over a saucepan to catch the juice, use a very sharp knife to cut between the membranes and remove the segments. Reserve the segments. Squeeze any juice out of the membrane into the pan. Add half the brandy and half the marmalade to the pan and heat gently to form a syrup.

Cut out a disc of baking parchment to fit the bottom of a 900 ml (1½ pint) pudding basin. Grease the basin and put the disc in the bottom. Add the orange and brandy syrup and leave to cool.

Cream the butter and sugar until white and fluffy. Gradually add the egg, beating well after each addition. Sift together the flour and salt. Using a metal spoon, gently fold half the flour into the creamed mixture, then fold in the remaining flour. Fold in the orange zest and gradually add enough milk to give a soft dropping consistency. Spoon into the basin.

Cover the basin with a piece of greased, pleated baking parchment and then a piece of pleated foil. Secure with string. Put into a saucepan and pour in enough boiling water to come halfway up the sides of the basin. Cover and steam for 1½–2 hours, topping up with boiling water if necessary. *(Continued on page 150.)*

Orange, Brandy and Marmalade Steamed Pudding

(Continued from page 148.) Meanwhile, make the sauce. Put the remaining marmalade and brandy in a saucepan and heat until just boiling. Add the orange segments and heat gently to warm through.

To serve, turn the pudding out of the basin and pour over the orange sauce.

BAKED RICE PUDDING

A deliciously rich and fruity version of this British classic.

INGREDIENTS FOR 4–6 SERVINGS

25 g (1 oz)	SULTANAS
25 g (1 oz)	RAISINS
1 tablespoon	DARK RUM
50 g (2 oz)	SHORT GRAIN RICE
300 ml (½ pint)	FULL-FAT MILK
300 ml (½ pint)	DOUBLE CREAM
2 tablespoons	SUGAR
¼ teaspoon	GROUND CINNAMON
	GRATED ZEST OF 1 LEMON
15 g (½ oz)	BUTTER, DICED

Put the sultanas and raisins into a bowl with the rum. Cover and leave to soak overnight.

Pre-heat the oven to 150C/300F/Gas 2. Butter a 1.1 litre (2 pint) ovenproof dish. Add the rice and soaked fruit. Warm the milk and the cream then pour over the rice. Sprinkle over the sugar, cinnamon and lemon zest and stir gently.

Dot with the butter and bake for 2–2½ hours. Serve.

VARIATION

Lemon Caramel Rice: Cook the pudding as above. Remove the skin. Mix 3 tablespoons lemon curd with 1 tablespoon water and drizzle over the pudding. Dust with icing sugar. Put under a pre-heated hot grill and grill until the lemon mixture has caramelized.

PEAR CHARLOTTE

A new version of this traditionally apple-based pudding – sweet fresh
pears layered with a lemony breadcrumb mix.

INGREDIENTS FOR 4–6 SERVINGS

75 g (3 oz) FRESH WHITE BREADCRUMBS
50 g (2 oz) VEGETABLE SUET
             GRATED ZEST OF 1 LEMON
75 g (3 oz) DEMERARA SUGAR
450 g (1 lb) PEARS
             STRAINED LEMON JUICE FOR SPRINKLING
25 g (1 oz) BUTTER, CHILLED

Pre-heat the oven to 180C/350F/Gas 4. Mix together the breadcrumbs, suet, lemon zest and demerara sugar. Peel, core and slice the pears.

Grease a deep ovenproof dish and add alternate layers of sliced pears and breadcrumb mixture, finishing with a layer of crumbs.

Sprinkle with a little lemon juice. Use a vegetable peeler to shave curls of butter on top of the pudding. Bake for 1 hour until the pears are tender and the topping golden. Serve with custard.

VARIATIONS

Any fruit that can be stewed works well in this dish; try apples, rhubarb or apple and blackberry.

BLACKBERRY AND APPLE CRUMBLE

A late-summer mix of fresh fruits cooked beneath a crunchy flapjack-style topping.

INGREDIENTS FOR 4–6 SERVINGS

450 g (1 lb) COOKING APPLES, PEELED, CORED AND SLICED
225 g (8 oz) BLACKBERRIES
25 g (1 oz) SOFT BROWN SUGAR

FOR THE TOPPING

100 g (4 oz) PLAIN FLOUR
100 g (4 oz) CASTER OR DEMERARA SUGAR
50 g (2 oz) ROLLED OATS
75 g (3 oz) UNSALTED BUTTER

Pre-heat the oven to 180C/350F/Gas 4. To make the topping, put the flour, sugar and oats in a bowl and rub in the butter.

Mix the apples and blackberries with the sugar and put in one large or four individual ovenproof dishes. Scatter over the topping.

Bake for 30–40 minutes until golden brown. Serve warm or cold with custard or clotted cream.

VARIATIONS

Replace the rolled oats in the topping with the same amount of muesli or nibbed almonds.

A variety of fruits can be used as the base of a crumble: gooseberry and ginger (add ½ teaspoon of ground ginger to the fruit and to the topping), mixed summer fruits, or pear and pineapple.

Tinned fruit can also be used – follow the recipe as above but you may not need to add any sugar. Reserve a little of the syrup and add to the custard to match the flavour of the crumble.

Crumble Pie: Line a flan tin with sweet pastry (see page 142) and bake blind. Fill with the fruit mixture, top with the crumble and bake as above.

Blackberry and Apple Crumble

BANANA AND APRICOT FRITTERS WITH BROWN BREAD ICE CREAM

The unusual nutty flavour of brown bread ice cream is the ideal accompaniment to these crisp-coated fruits.

INGREDIENTS FOR 4 SERVINGS

2	BANANAS
4	APRICOTS
50 g (2 oz)	PLAIN FLOUR
	VEGETABLE OIL FOR DEEP FRYING
	BROWN BREAD ICE CREAM (SEE PAGE 156), TO SERVE
	ICING SUGAR FOR DUSTING
	CINNAMON STICKS, TO DECORATE

FOR THE BATTER

100 g (4 oz)	PLAIN FLOUR
	PINCH OF SALT
1	EGG
150 ml (¼ pint)	MILK
25 g (1 oz)	BUTTER, MELTED

To make the batter, sift the flour and salt into a bowl. Beat the egg into the milk. Make a well in the flour and pour in the milk and egg mixture. Whisk the liquid to gradually incorporate the flour and form a smooth batter. Whisk in the melted butter. Leave to stand while you prepare the fruit.

Peel the bananas and cut each one into four even-sized pieces. Carefully peel the apricots, cut in half and remove the stone.

Heat the oil in a deep-fat fryer or large saucepan to 180C/350F. Lightly coat the fruit with the flour. Dip the fruit into the batter, draining off any excess, then lower into the hot oil and cook for 2–3 minutes until golden brown. Cook in batches if necessary. Drain well, place on kitchen paper to absorb any excess fat and keep warm while frying the remainder.

Serve with a generous helping of brown bread ice cream, decorated with curls of cinnamon and dusted with icing sugar.

Banana and Apricot Fritters with Brown Bread Ice Cream

BROWN BREAD ICE CREAM

You will not need all of this ice cream to accompany the fruit fritters (see page 154), but you can store the rest in the freezer.

COOKING TIP

If you have an ice cream maker, this will certainly reduce the preparation time. Refer to the manufacturer's instructions as to when to add the caramelized breadcrumbs.

INGREDIENTS FOR 8 SERVINGS

50 g (2 oz) FRESH WHOLEMEAL BREADCRUMBS
50 g (2 oz) SOFT BROWN SUGAR
600 ml (1 pint) WHIPPING CREAM

FOR THE SYRUP

100 g (4 oz) CASTER SUGAR
4 tablespoons WATER

Pre-heat the grill. Spread the breadcrumbs on a baking sheet and sprinkle with the sugar. Grill until the sugar has melted and the breadcrumbs are a dark golden colour. Leave to cool.

When completely cold, crush the breadcrumb mixture with a pestle and mortar or in a food processor. Set aside.

To make the syrup, put the sugar and water into a small saucepan and heat gently until the sugar has completely dissolved. Continue to heat for 3 minutes then remove from the heat and leave to cool.

Pour the cold syrup and cream into a mixing bowl and whisk with an electric whisk until the mixture thickens (to a consistency like whipped cream). Pour the mixture into a 2.3 litre (4 pint) freezerproof plastic container, cover and freeze for 3 hours.

When the edges of the ice-cream are frozen but the centre still soft, remove from the freezer, transfer to a bowl and whisk thoroughly until smooth. Return to the container, cover and freeze for 3–4 hours. Remove from the freezer and whisk again. Fold in the caramelized breadcrumbs. Return to the container, cover and freeze until firm.

To serve the ice-cream, transfer to the refrigerator 30 minutes before serving, to allow it to soften a little.

FESTIVE PINWHEELS

No festive table would be complete without a mince pie. Try this new version to surprise your guests at Christmas.

INGREDIENTS FOR 10 SERVINGS

450 g (1 lb) MINCEMEAT
          ICING SUGAR FOR DUSTING

FOR THE SHORTCRUST PASTRY

225 g (8 oz) PLAIN FLOUR
100 g (4 oz) BUTTER OR MARGARINE
2–3 tablespoons COLD WATER

FOR THE PINWHEELS

225 g (8 oz) PUFF PASTRY
175 g (6 oz) MARZIPAN

To make the shortcrust pastry, sift the flour into a bowl, add the butter or margarine and rub in until the mixture resembles fine breadcrumbs. Add sufficient cold water to form a smooth dough. Wrap in cling film and chill for 30 minutes.

Pre-heat the oven to 200C/400F/Gas 6. Roll out the pastry on a lightly floured surface and use to line a 25 cm (10 inch) pie plate. Spread the mincemeat evenly over the pastry base.

To make the pinwheels, roll out the puff pastry to a rectangle 25 x 30 cm (10 x 12 inches). Roll out the marzipan to the same size. Put the marzipan on top of the pastry and roll up.

Cut the roll into 1 cm (½ inch) slices, put the slices on their side and flatten slightly. Arrange the pinwheels over the mincemeat so that all the filling is covered. Bake for about 30 minutes until golden brown.

Dust with icing sugar and serve with brandy butter, custard, ice cream or brandy sauce.

AFTERNOON TEA

BANANA, HONEY AND HAZELNUT LOAF

Adding bananas to a cake gives it a rich flavour and texture. The chopped nuts and sugar topping add a little crunch.

INGREDIENTS

6 tablespoons	CLEAR HONEY
225 g (8 oz)	SELF-RAISING FLOUR
100 g (4 oz)	SOFT MARGARINE
3	RIPE BANANAS, MASHED
75 g (3 oz)	MUSCOVADO SUGAR
3	EGGS
50 g (2 oz)	CHOPPED HAZELNUTS
	SUGAR CUBES, TO DECORATE

Pre-heat the oven to 180C/350F/Gas 4. Grease a 900 g (2 lb) loaf tin and line the base with baking parchment.

Reserve 2 tablespoons of the honey, then put the remainder of the honey in a bowl with all the other ingredients except the sugar cubes. Beat together until well combined. Pour the mixture into the prepared tin.

Bake for about 1 hour. To test that the cake is cooked, insert a skewer into the centre of cake, if it comes out clean the cake is ready. Allow the cake to cool in the tin for 5 minutes. Turn out, remove the baking parchment and leave to cool on a wire rack.

To finish the cake, heat the reserved honey until melted and brush over the loaf. Crush the sugar cubes and sprinkle over the cake. Leave to cool, slice and serve.

Overleaf (clockwise from top):
Rich Sherry and
Almond Cake;
Traditional Tea
Bread; Clotted
Cream Bread and
Butter Slice; Scones;
Banana, Honey
and Hazelnut Loaf;
Cherry Frangipans;
Malt Loaf.

RICH SHERRY AND ALMOND CAKE

A light cake delicately flavoured with almonds and sherry.

INGREDIENTS

225 g (8 oz)	BUTTER
225 g (8 oz)	CASTER SUGAR
4	EGGS (SIZE 4), BEATEN
225 g (8 oz)	SELF-RAISING FLOUR
175 g (6 oz)	GROUND ALMONDS
6 tablespoons	SWEET SHERRY
1 teaspoon	ALMOND ESSENCE
25 g (1 oz)	FLAKED ALMONDS
	ICING SUGAR FOR DUSTING (OPTIONAL)

> **COOKING TIP**
> It is not vital to base-line the cake tin, especially if the tin is non-stick, but it does guarantee easy removal.

Pre-heat the oven to 170C/325F/Gas 3. Grease a 20 cm (8 inch) loose-bottomed deep cake tin and line the base with baking parchment.

Cream together the butter and sugar until white and fluffy. Gradually add the eggs, a little at a time, beating well between each addition. Gently fold in the flour and ground almonds and then the sherry and almond essence. Turn the mixture into the prepared tin and sprinkle with the flaked almonds.

Bake for about 1 hour. To test that the cake is cooked, insert a skewer into the centre of cake, if it comes out clean the cake is ready. Allow the cake to cool in the tin for 5 minutes. Turn out, remove the baking parchment and leave to cool on a wire rack.

Dust liberally with icing sugar, if liked, before serving.

SCONES

*So quick to make, these scones are ideal for unexpected guests
at tea-time.*

SERVING TIP
For an indulgent
tea-time treat,
serve plain scones
with a dollop of
clotted cream and
home-made
strawberry jam.

INGREDIENTS FOR 10–12 SCONES

225 g (8 oz) SELF-RAISING FLOUR

1 teaspoon BAKING POWDER

50 g (2 oz) BLOCK MARGARINE

about 150 ml (¼ pint) MILK

BEATEN EGG FOR GLAZING

Pre-heat the oven to 220C/425F/Gas 7. Sift the flour and baking
powder into a bowl, add the margarine and rub into the flour until
the mixtures resembles fine breadcrumbs. Add enough milk to bind
to a smooth dough. Knead lightly. Roll out on a lightly floured
surface until 2 cm (¾ inch) thick and cut out 5 cm (2 inch) rounds
with a pastry cutter.

Brush the tops of the scones with beaten egg and transfer to a
baking sheet. Bake for about 10 minutes until golden brown.
Transfer to a wire rack and leave to cool slightly. Serve warm.

VARIATIONS

There are many variations on the basic scone recipe. Add the extra
ingredients after you have rubbed the margarine into the flour, then
continue as above.

Cranberry and Sultana Scones: Add 25 g (1 oz) dried cranberries
and 50 g (2 oz) sultanas.

Cheese Scones: Add 50 g (2 oz) grated mature Cheddar cheese
and 1 teaspoon of mustard powder.

Date Scones: Add 50 g (2 oz) chopped dates.

Cranberry and Sultana Scones

EARL GREY CAKE

The slightly smoky flavour of Earl Grey tea lends a really distinctive taste to this unusual new cake.

INGREDIENTS

225 g (8 oz) CASTER SUGAR
225 g (8 oz) BUTTER
3 EGGS (SIZE 4), BEATEN
250 g (9 oz) SELF-RAISING FLOUR
50 ml (2 fl oz) STRONG COLD EARL GREY TEA

Pre-heat the oven to 170C/325F/Gas 3. Grease a 20 cm (8 inch) loose-bottomed deep cake tin and line the base with baking parchment.

Cream together the butter and sugar until white and fluffy. Gradually add the eggs, a little at a time, beating well between each addition. Gently fold in the flour and then the Earl Grey tea. Turn the mixture into the prepared tin.

Bake for about 40 minutes. To test that the cake is cooked, insert a skewer into the centre of the cake, if it comes out clean the cake is ready. Allow to cool in the tin for 5 minutes. Turn out, remove the baking parchment and leave to cool on a wire rack.

MALT LOAF

Make your own malt loaf and find out just how good it can be.

INGREDIENTS

8 tablespoons	MALT EXTRACT
75 ml (3 fl oz)	STRONG HOT TEA
175 g (6 oz)	WHOLEMEAL SELF-RAISING FLOUR
75 g (3 oz)	RAISINS
75 g (3 oz)	SULTANAS
1	EGG (SIZE 4)

> **BUYING TIP**
> You can buy pure malt extract from a chemist or health food shop. It is quite expensive but will make a malt loaf far superior to any of the commercial varieties.

Stir the malt extract into the hot tea and leave to cool. Pre-heat the oven to 140C/275F/Gas 1. Grease a 900 g (2 lb) loaf tin and line the base with baking parchment.

Put the flour, fruits, egg and cooled malt mixture into a bowl and mix well. Turn the mixture into the prepared loaf tin.

Bake for 1–1½ hours. To test that the loaf is cooked, insert a skewer into the centre of the loaf, if it comes out clean the loaf is ready. Allow the loaf to cool in the tin for 5 minutes. Turn out, remove the baking parchment and leave to cool on a wire rack.

When completely cold, wrap in clean baking parchment and store in an airtight container for 3–4 days before serving.

CLOTTED CREAM BREAD AND BUTTER SLICE

This wicked pastry is quite irresistible. Just don't count the calories!

INGREDIENTS FOR 4–6 SERVINGS

2	SOFT WHITE ROLLS
50 g (2 oz)	BUTTER, SOFTENED
50 g (2 oz)	RAISINS
4	EGGS (SIZE 4)
75 g (3 oz)	CASTER SUGAR
100 ml (4 fl oz)	FULL-FAT MILK
200 ml (7 fl oz)	DOUBLE CREAM
100 ml (4 fl oz)	CLOTTED CREAM
1	VANILLA POD

FOR THE PASTRY

175 g (6 oz)	PLAIN FLOUR
75 g (3 oz)	BUTTER
1 tablespoon	CASTER SUGAR
	PINCH OF SALT
1	EGG, BEATEN

FOR THE GLAZE

2 tablespoons	APRICOT JAM
1 tablespoon	WATER

To make the pastry, sift the flour into a bowl and rub in the butter until the mixture resembles fine breadcrumbs. Stir in the sugar and salt. Add the egg and mix to form a smooth dough. Wrap in cling film and chill for 30 minutes.

Pre-heat the oven to 200C/400F/Gas 6. Roll out the pastry on a lightly floured surface and use to line a 20 cm (8 inch) flan tin. Line with baking parchment and fill with dried peas or beans. Bake blind for 15 minutes. Leave to cool.

Reduce the oven temperature to 140C/275F/Gas 1. Thinly slice the bread rolls and spread on one side with the butter. Arrange one layer of bread, butter side up, in the pastry case, then sprinkle with raisins. Add the remaining bread. *(Continued on page 168.)*

Clotted Cream Bread and Butter Slice

(Continued from page 166.) Beat together the eggs and sugar. Put the milk, creams and vanilla pod in a small saucepan and heat gently, stirring, until just on the point of boiling. Remove the vanilla pod and stir the milk mixture into the eggs and sugar. Strain and carefully ladle over the bread slices. Bake for 30–35 minutes.

To make the glaze, put the apricot jam and water in a small saucepan and heat gently until the jam melts. Press through a sieve and brush over the flan while it is still warm. Serve the flan warm with vanilla ice cream and cinnamon sugar.

TRADITIONAL TEA BREAD

There are many different regional recipes for tea breads. This version uses self-raising flour to make it rise rather than yeast.

INGREDIENTS

175 g (6 oz) CURRANTS
75 g (3 oz) SULTANAS
75 g (3 oz) RAISINS
225 g (8 oz) CASTER SUGAR
300 ml (½ pint) STRONG HOT TEA
275 g (10 oz) SELF-RAISING FLOUR
1 EGG (SIZE 4), BEATEN

Put the fruits and sugar in a bowl and cover with the hot tea. Leave to cool. Pre-heat the oven to 150C/300F/Gas 2. Grease a 900 g (2 lb) loaf tin and line the base with baking parchment.

Add the flour and egg to the fruit and tea mixture, mixing well. Pour into the prepared tin.

Bake for about 1½ hours. To test that the loaf is cooked, insert a skewer into the centre of the loaf, if it comes out clean the loaf is ready. Allow to cool in the tin for 5 minutes. Turn out, remove the baking parchment and leave to cool on a wire rack.

Serve sliced and buttered.

CHERRY FRANGIPANS

*These delightful individual tartlets contain an almond filling
studded with fresh ripe cherries.*

INGREDIENTS FOR 4 SERVINGS
FOR THE PASTRY

225 g (8 oz) PLAIN FLOUR
150 g (5 oz) BUTTER, SOFTENED
1 EGG, BEATEN

FOR THE FRANGIPAN

50 g (2 oz) BUTTER, SOFTENED
50 g (2 oz) CASTER SUGAR
1 EGG (SIZE 4), BEATEN
50 g (2 oz) GROUND ALMONDS
15 g ($\frac{1}{2}$ oz) SELF-RAISING FLOUR
175 g (6 oz) CHERRIES, STONED

FOR THE GLAZE

2 tablespoons APRICOT JAM
1 tablespoon WATER

To make the pastry, break the butter into small pieces and whisk
into the egg. Add the flour and mix to form a smooth dough. Wrap
in cling film and chill for 30 minutes.

Lightly butter four 7.5 cm (3 inch) flan tins. Roll out the pastry
on a lightly floured surface. Cut out rounds of pastry and ease them
into the tins. Prick lightly with a fork and chill for 30 minutes. Pre-
heat the oven to 190C/375F/Gas 5.

To make the frangipan, cream together the butter and sugar
until white and fluffy. Gradually add the egg, a little at a time,
beating well after each addition. Fold in the almonds and flour.

Three-quarters fill each pastry case with the frangipan. Press the
cherries into the mixture and bake for about 15 minutes or until the
frangipan springs back when lightly pressed.

Remove from the tins and transfer to a wire rack. To make the
glaze, put the jam and water in a small saucepan and heat gently
until the jam melts. Press through a sieve and brush over the tartlets
while they are still warm. Leave to cool slightly before serving.

BRITISH CHEESES

CHOOSING CHEESE

We have included a wide variety of British cheeses in this chapter. Some may be more familiar than others, but all should be available from a cheesemonger or good delicatessen; if they don't stock the one you want, then ask, they should be able to get it for you. For the more common cheeses, it is worth seeking the farmhouse-produced versions as they tend to be matured for longer and thus have more flavour.

When choosing cheese, taste before you buy if possible. Loosely wrap the cheese in greaseproof paper or foil and keep in a cool larder or in the least cold part of your refrigerator. Remember to remove it from the refrigerator an hour or two before serving, to allow the cheese to return to room temperature and recover its full flavour, which will have been dulled by chilling.

THE CHEESE BOARD

Selecting the cheese for your cheese board when entertaining is very much like menu planning – you should visualise what it is going to look like. The cheeses you select need to be well balanced in terms of colour, texture and flavour. As a general rule, a cheese board for a dinner party should consist of up to five cheeses, including one that is mild, one tasty but not too strong, and one that is richly aromatic and flavoursome. Serve only medium-sized pieces of cheese – allow 25–50 g (1–2 oz) per person – no one will eat much after a filling main course. Serve each cheese with its own knife to prevent cross flavouring.

At a buffet or a wine and cheese party, you will obviously serve a wider variety of cheeses, but don't be tempted to go overboard, it is better to offer a few larger pieces than a lot of small ones.

Serve the cheese with a selection of biscuits, such as crackers and oatcakes, and crisp sticks of celery or fruit such as grapes, which not only serve as a colourful garnish for the cheese board, but also taste good when eaten with the cheese.

Here are four ideas for well balanced British cheese boards that will give your guests a taste of what Britain has to offer. As has been stressed throughout the book, these are only ideas to inspire you, do try your own combinations.

Overleaf: A selection of British cheeses

GREAT BRITISH CHEESE BOARD

This is a good, varied selection of cheeses, some of which are a little out of the ordinary, for a cheeseboard with a difference.

BLUE VINNEY

Similar to Stilton in appearance, though not as sharp and with considerably more veining. The genuine article, made according to traditional methods, comes only from Woodbridge Farm, near Sturminster Newton in Dorset, and is also known as Dorset Blue. As with most hand-made cheeses, the appearance and taste can vary slightly. Less authentic but good quality versions, produced elsewhere, are quite widely available.

MATURE FARMHOUSE CHEDDAR

First produced in the Middle Ages, real farmhouse Cheddar is now made in less than 20 farms in the South-West of England and is a very different product to the mass-produced Cheddar found in your local supermarket. It is golden yellow in colour and close textured with a strong, nutty taste.

SHARPHAM

This is a soft, rinded cheese like Brie or Camembert. It is made in Devon from unpasteurized jersey milk and vegetarian rennet. Mild and buttery to taste, it is matured for 6 weeks.

VULSCOMBE

A rich, smooth and creamy goat's milk cheese from Tiverton in Devon. It is matured for about 3 weeks and is available plain or flavoured with fresh herbs or with crushed peppercorns and garlic.

CABOC

A rich, double cream cheese made from the cream of cow's milk and rolled in crunchy oatmeal. It was first made in the Western highlands of Scotland in the fifteenth century.

TRADITIONAL CHEESE BOARD

A cheeseboard full of classics bound to be popular with everyone.

MATURE FARMHOUSE CHEDDAR

A traditional British cheese board just wouldn't be complete without this great classic. Real farmhouse Cheddar is a very different product to the mass-produced Cheddar found in your local supermarket. It is golden yellow in colour and close textured with a strong, nutty taste.

STILTON

The 'king' of British cheeses, made in the counties of Leicestershire, Derbyshire and Nottinghamshire. The creamy ivory paste is marbled with greenish-blue veins and its flavour ranges from mild with a sharp edge when young, to rich and tangy when mature.

SOMERSET BRIE

A rich, smooth, creamy cheese, with the traditional white bloomy rind. The rind is edible and the centre should have a soft, springy texture – if it is chalky the cheese is not yet ripe.

GOAT'S CHEESE PYRAMID

A semi-hard cheese with the characteristic tangy flavour of goat's milk. It is moulded into a distinctive pyramid shape which is easily cut into slices for serving.

LEICESTER

Sometimes unnecessarily called Red Leicester (there is no other kind). This bright russet-gold to tomato-red coloured cheese has a mellow, nutty flavour with a faint lemony taste and moist texture.

Traditional Cheese Board

CLASSIC CHEESE BOARD

An unusual selection of specialist British cheeses.

WELLINGTON

Produced from cow's milk from the Duke of Wellington's herd of Guernsey cattle. A cheese that is deep golden in colour, close textured, and with a delicately sweet flavour and fruity aroma.

SHROPSHIRE BLUE

An orange-coloured cheese with even blue veining extending from the centre. Produced from cow's milk. It has a slightly milder flavour than Stilton.

SMOKED WEDMORE

A type of small Caerphilly, from Somerset. It has a layer of fresh chives in the centre and is lightly smoked.

SHARPHAM MINI

A soft, Camembert-type cheese made in Devon from Jersey milk and vegetarian rennet. A mild, buttery cheese.

TORNEGUS

Made as Caerphilly in Somerset, then transferred to Surrey where it is washed with Kentish wine. It has an orange rind and a springy texture which becomes softer around the edges. The strong flavour is fruity when the cheese is young, but becomes more pungent as the cheese matures.

CHRISTMAS CHEESE BOARD

The finest of British cheeses that are at their best at Christmas.

HALF BABY STILTON

Traditionally served at Christmas because the best Stilton is made with summer milk, which gives the cheese a slightly yellow paste. When buying Stilton, look for one with evenly distributed veins and a good contrast between the creamy paste and the blue veins. As the Stilton ages, the mould spreads and the flavour deepens, although the rate varies from one cheese to another. Stilton is an excellent dessert cheese accompanied by a glass of port.

CHEDDAR TRUCKLE

A truckle is a small cheese, usually weighing between 1.8 kg (4 lb) and 4.5 kg (10 lb), and wrapped in cloth or coated in wax. A small truckle of Cheddar is ideal to last through the Christmas season of entertaining. Mature Cheddar is ripened for at least 5 months, and perhaps as many as 18. It is best to buy truckles that have been matured for as long as possible, to obtain that distinctive mellow and nutty flavour with the golden yellow colour.

BABY CORNISH YARG

An impressive looking cheese coated in nettle leaves which give it a slightly herby taste. It is similar to Wensleydale in that it is moist and crumbly, but it is a mould-ripened cheese which develops a creamier texture from the outside in. It is sold at 3–6 weeks old.

BELLE D'ECOSSE

A Camembert-style cheese made from March to December in the Borders area of Scotland. Made with unpasteurized milk, Belle d'Ecosse is a lightly pressed cheese which softens as it ripens. White moulds with light brown flecks coat the surface. The cheese ripens over 4–5 weeks, becoming deep yellow with a pronounced flavour.

CELTIC PROMISE

An unpasteurized farmhouse cheese made at Glynhynod farm in Dyfed, Wales. The cheese is washed in cider to give the rind a golden brown hue.

ENTERTAINING

INSPIRED ENTERTAINING

The aim of this book is to recreate classic British dishes and make them more accessible to the modern-day cook. In the busy lives we lead today there is little time for the lengthy preparation often needed for traditional dishes, so wherever possible the recipes include short cuts and time-saving tips. This chapter on entertaining is written in a similar vein, to help you organize your valuable time and make entertaining as pleasurable for you as it is for your guests – a stressful cook only creates a tense atmosphere. The suggested menus cover a variety of events, including a festive menu that can be served as a Christmas dinner or for any other special occasion.

Planning is vital to stress-free entertaining. Consider how much time you have and plan the menu accordingly, thinking of ways to cut corners if necessary. Give yourself plenty of time: deciding on your menu only the night before limits your choice and means an exhausting day spent both shopping and cooking. Here are some points you should consider before entertaining.

THEME

Every entertaining event has a theme; a dinner party or lunch party is a theme. As the starting point to your entertaining, decide what the theme is going to be and use it as the basis for the whole event – the menu, wine, table settings, etc.

GUESTS

Decide on the guests, write or telephone with your invitations if needed and confirm the final numbers. Remember to find out if there are any vegetarian or other special diets to be catered for.

MENU

Devise your menu. There are certain key points to consider when menu planning:

The appearance of the food. Colours should be well balanced and pleasing to the eye, not bland and certainly not overdone. A well chosen garnish or decoration can help enhance bland colours or tone down strong colours. Don't forget the colours of the china too, food can sometimes get lost among the patterns of multi-coloured plates.

The texture of the food. There should be a variety of textures, not just between the items on the plate but also the courses.

Overleaf: Mustard Roast Gammon with a Peach Sauce

Availability of ingredients. Although many ingredients are now available throughout the year, the cost and quality will vary, so it is best to plan your menu to include foods that are in season.

Your kitchen. One aspect of menu planning which is not immediately obvious is the availability of equipment and space in your kitchen. You need to be sure that you have sufficient oven and hob space for what you intend to cook and also that your refrigerator is large enough to store it. Also consider if any recipes require special equipment that you may not have.

Confidence. Take the stress out of entertaining by including dishes that you are confident about preparing and cooking. If you'd like to try something new but feel unsure about it, practise before the event. Adapt recipes if possible – dishes that appear complex may be made simpler by replacing some of the ingredients with ready-prepared ones, such as frozen pastry.

Time. Decide how much time you are going to have to prepare the meal. Whether you have two hours after work or two whole days will determine the dishes you choose.

SHOPPING

Write a shopping list, dividing it, if you like, into the key shops – butcher, grocer, greengrocer and baker. This saves time and ensures you don't forget anything. Remember to include any non-food items such as napkins and table decorations. If it is a special occasion such as Christmas, consider when you will need to buy the ingredients – both for the dishes you can prepare in advance and to ensure the foods are at their best. You may also need to consider when the shops are going to be closed.

TIME PLAN

It can also be of benefit to draw up a time plan. The plan may only be simple, eg, prepare this and that today and the rest in the morning; others can detail specific times and events leading up to the serving of the first course. Make sure you don't cut the times too tight – you need to allow for the unexpected, especially at Christmas when friends may pop in for a drink and a mince pie!

Preparing food in advance can help ease the work load on the day. Many dishes can be at least part prepared, with just the finishing touches added before serving. Use your freezer if you have one, but don't forget to allow time for defrosting.

Now you know how to do it, let's entertain!

SUMMER'S EVENING MENU

This is a menu of glorious summer colours and flavours that doesn't demand too much work at the end of a warm summer's day.

GOLDEN VEGETABLE SOUP
❖
RED MULLET WITH CARAMELIZED ONIONS AND GOOSEBERRY PUREE
GARDEN SALAD WITH CIDER DRESSING
WARM NEW POTATO SALAD
❖
SUMMER PUDDINGS
CREAM

TIMING AND TIPS

The summer pudding should be made the day before, to allow the bread to soak up all the juices of the fruit.

Prepare the vegetables for the soup in advance; it is worth spending some time cutting the vegetables into neat shapes as it will enhance the appearance of the soup. If you have it, use a home-made vegetable or chicken stock. The soup only needs 15 minutes cooking time – be careful not to overcook it as the vegetables will lose their shape and the soup its colour and texture.

Prepare the gooseberry purée and caramelized onions for the fish dish before sitting down to the first course, but the fish only takes 5–6 minutes to cook, so is best done after the first course; the fish will be hot and cooked to perfection.

Prepare the green salad leaves and dressing separately in advance, and toss together just before serving.

Cook and slice the potatoes for the potato salad just before dinner and keep warm. As with the green salad, mix with the dressing just before serving.

CLASSIC DINNER PARTY

A special menu of richly flavoured dishes for a leisurely dinner party.

SPINACH AND CAERPHILLY TERRINE

❖

MUSSELS WITH CREAM AND ROSEMARY

❖

GUINEA FOWL WITH FENNEL

NEW POTATOES

LEEKS WITH MUSTARD BUTTER

❖

BREAD AND BUTTER PUDDING

TIMING AND TIPS

The spinach terrine is served cold so can be made in advance of the dinner and stored in the refrigerator until you are ready to serve it. It looks good served whole, so impress your guests and turn it out on to a long serving plate and slice it at the table.

The mussels are simple to prepare and quick to cook. Prepare all the ingredients in advance and put in the refrigerator. Simply cook them after the first course so they are as fresh as possible.

The guinea fowl needs to be marinated for at least 4 hours so this can be prepared well ahead of the dinner party. Put in the oven 15 minutes before sitting down to the first course so that it will be perfectly cooked in time for serving.

Alter the vegetables according to the season.

You may consider a bread and butter pudding to be a rather heavy ending to this meal but this version is deliciously light and creamy and you need only serve it in small portions.

SUMMER-TIME LUNCH

A light, refreshing meal perfect for eating oudoors on a beautiful sunny day.

SMOKED CHICKEN AND AVOCADO SOUP

❖

ROASTED SALMON TROUT WITH STIR-FRIED VEGETABLES

❖

RIPE TART

RASPBERRY SORBET

TIMING AND TIPS

The soup is chilled so is best made the day before. The garnish for the soup needs to be cooked just before serving so that it retains its crispness, but if you prefer, simply finish the soup with a sprinkling of snipped chives instead.

Prepare the vegetables for the fish dish in advance. The butter sauce can be made before sitting down for the soup and kept warm, but it is best to cook the fish immediately before serving as it is easy to overcook it and spoil its delicate flavour. Stir-fry the vegetables while the fish is in the oven.

The ripe tart can be prepared and cooked in advance. It's delicious served on its own but if you prefer, buy a good quality raspberry sorbet as an accompaniment, or serve with cream.

SUNDAY LUNCH

*Treat your family and friends to this stunning array of classic
British dishes for a traditional Sunday lunch.*

POACHED PEARS WITH STILTON
❖
BRAISED DEVON ROAST
FANTAIL POTATOES
CAULIFLOWER WITH THREE-CHEESE SAUCE
SPRING GREENS WITH APPLE
❖
TREACLE TART
CUSTARD

TIMING AND TIPS

Prepare and poach the pears in advance and make the Stilton
filling, then refrigerate until just before the meal. Grill the pears just
before serving.

The braised beef makes a simple but tasty alternative to the
more traditional roast. It requires 2 hours cooking time so once it is
in the oven you can prepare the pudding. Make the treacle tart and
leave to cool.

Prepare the vegetables. Time the cooking of the vegetables so
they are ready to serve with the roast – they will deteriorate if kept
for too long.

The roast can be carved and arranged on a serving dish then
coated with the sauce and kept warm until required. Alternatively,
carve it at the table and serve the sauce separately.

When you sit down to the main course, put the treacle tart in
the oven to warm through before serving.

FESTIVE DINNER

A delightful menu suitable for serving at any kind of celebration get-together.

SOMERSET BRIE AND SMOKED SALMON PARCELS
❖
MUSTARD ROAST GAMMON WITH A PEACH SAUCE
ROAST POTATOES
NEEPS AND TATTIES
ROAST PARSNIPS WITH HONEY
BROAD BEANS WITH PARSLEY SAUCE
STEAMED BRUSSELS SPROUTS
❖
FESTIVE PINWHEELS
❖
CHRISTMAS CHEESE BOARD

TIMING AND TIPS

Put the gammon to soak in the morning.

Boil the gammon and leave to cool. If you intend to serve the gammon cold it can be roasted in advance, but it is just as easy to cook it at the same time as you roast the vegetables

Prepare and cook the festive pinwheels in advance and leave to cool. Prepare the Brie and salmon parcels but don't coat with breadcrumbs. Store in the refrigerator and breadcrumb just before cooking and serving.

Remove the cheeses from the refrigerator and loosely cover about 1 hour before serving, to allow them to come to room temperature and 'breathe'. This brings out their full flavours.

The neeps and tatties can be finished before you sit down to the starter and kept warm. Time the roasting of the potatoes and parsnips so they will be ready to serve with the main course. Cook the broad beans and parsley sauce and keep warm. Pour the sauce over the beans just before serving.

The gammon looks so impressive it is best to carve it at the table. Employ a volunteer to carve so you are free to finish the vegetables and prepare the sauce.

When you sit down to the main course, put the pinwheels in the oven to warm through before serving.

GREAT BRITISH BUFFET

Many buffets consist of cold foods eaten with the fingers, but hot buffets work just as well and, if you choose the dishes carefully, can be eaten with just a fork.

LADY LLANOVER'S SALT DUCK WITH PICKLED DAMSONS

POTTED CHEESE WITH HERBS

WALNUT BREAD

❖

IRISH STEW

SMOKED FISH PIE

RUNNER BEANS WITH TOMATOES AND HERBS

SEASONAL LEAF SALAD

❖

STRAWBERRIES AND CREAM WITH CHOCOLATE SHORTBREAD

BURNT CAMBRIDGE CREAMS

❖

GREAT BRITISH CHEESE BOARD

TIMING AND TIPS

Begin preparing the duck 3 days in advance. Make the pickled damsons at the same time.

On the day of the buffet, prepare the Cambridge creams and chill. Cook the salt duck and leave to cool. Prepare the potted cheese and make the chocolate shortbread in advance. About 30 minutes before serving, spread the potted cheese on the walnut bread and assemble the chocolate shortbreads.

The Irish stew will take 2–2½ hours to cook, so time the preparation and cooking so it can be taken straight from the oven. Make it in an attractive casserole so it can be served straight from the pot. The fish pie takes 30 minutes to cook so time it so it is ready at the same time as the stew. It needs to be served straight from the dish, so make sure the dish is presentable!

Remove the cheese from the refrigerator and cover loosely about 1 hour before serving.

Your guests may linger over the courses so don't be too strict on timing – the hot dishes will keep warm without being spoilt.

GLOSSARY OF TERMS

BAKE BLIND

To bake blind is to cook a pastry case before adding a filling, to ensure the pastry stays crisp. Preheat the oven to 200C/400F/Gas 6. Line the tin with the pastry, then put a piece of baking parchment into the pastry case and fill the case with dried peas or beans. If the filling is to be cooked inside the case, part-bake the pastry for 15 minutes, until just set. If the filling requires no further baking, the pastry should be fully cooked for a total of 20–25 minutes, until golden. The beans weigh down the pastry and prevent it rising – special ceramic baking beans can be bought, but dried beans or peas, or even uncooked rice, are just as good.

BASTE

To spoon the cooking juices and melted fat over meat or poultry during roasting or grilling, which prevents the meat from drying out. If roasting a joint of meat or a bird, baste every 15–30 minutes.

BLANCH

To immerse in boiling water for a short time. Blanched foods are often immediately rinsed in cold water or plunged into a bowl of iced water to prevent further cooking. Blanching vegetables before further cooking helps retain their colour. Blanching tomatoes and fruit such as peaches loosens the skin and makes them easy to peel. Blanching also refers to the initial frying of the potatoes when making chips.

CARAMELIZE

To cook sugar until it turns brown and becomes toffee-like. Foods that contain sugar, such as apples, onions and parsnips, can also be caramelized – the heat of cooking turns their sugars brown and gives them a sweet, sticky coating.

CROUTONS

Cubes of crisp fried or toasted bread sprinkled over soups or salads just before serving. Fried croûtons stay crisp longer than toasted ones.

DARIOLE MOULD

A small, rounded metal or plastic mould with a flat base, about the size of a tea cup. It is used for making small, individual puddings and desserts, which are turned out before serving.

DEGLAZE

To add a liquid, such as wine or stock, to a pan that has been used to cook meat or poultry. It loosens the sediment that sticks to the pan and adds extra flavour and colour to the sauce.

FLAKE

To separate cooked fish into its natural flakes. It is best done with a fork, exerting only a little pressure.

GRIDDLE

A flat, heavy metal plate used on top of the cooker when making drop scones or griddle scones, etc.

GRILL PAN

A flat, cast-iron pan with a ridged surface. It is brushed lightly with oil and heated until very hot before adding the food. It gives a charred effect to food cooked on it, similar to that of a barbecue. Food cooked in this way is described as char-grilled.

INFUSING

A method of adding ingredients to a liquid so that they add their flavour, eg infusing milk with a vanilla pod, or oil with a garlic clove. The liquid is sometimes heated to bring out more flavour, left to stand for about 30 minutes, then strained before use.

MARINATING

Soaking meat or poultry in a flavoured liquor (marinade) to increase tenderness and add flavour. A marinade usually includes an oil, to keep the food moist, and an acid such as lemon juice or vinegar, which tenderizes the food.

QUENELLE

The oval shape produced when food is moulded using two dessertspoons. It is used to improve the presentation of foods such as puréed vegetables, ice creams, sorbets and mousses.

RAMEKIN

A small, round ovenproof dish, used for making individual servings of pâté, puddings, etc.

REDUCE

To boil a liquid so that water evaporates from it to produce a smaller volume of liquid with a more concentrated flavour. Reducing a liquid also often thickens it.

RUB IN

To blend flour and fat, such as butter or margarine, when making pastry, scones, etc. Use the fingertips to rub together the ingredients until the texture resembles fine breadcrumbs. For best results, the fat should be chilled.

SCORE

To mark or cut the surface of food (usually joints of meat) to improve the appearance and/or cooking time. Use a sharp knife and, when scoring skin, rind or fat, be sure not to cut through to the meat.

SKIM

To remove impurities, such as froth, scum or fat, from the surface of a stock, gravy or stew, either during or after cooking.

SWEAT

To gently cook foods such as vegetables, usually in butter or oil, to allow them to cook in their own steam until they soften but do not brown.

TERRINE

A deep, rectangular dish, traditionally made from earthenware, which is used for cooking dishes such as pâtés. A loaf tin may also be used.

TURN

To trim vegetables such as carrots into barrel shapes.

ZEST

The coloured layer of the peel of citrus fruits. When paring the zest from an orange or lemon be sure to leave behind the bitter-tasting pith.

INDEX